Old Testament
Commentary
Survey

Old Testament Commentary Survey

FIFTH EDITION

Tremper Longman III

Baker Academic
a division of Baker Publishing Group
Grand Rapids, Michigan

© 1991, 1995, 2003, 2007, 2013 by Tremper Longman III

Published by Baker Academic
a division of Baker Publishing Group
P.O. Box 6287, Grand Rapids, MI 49516-6287
www.bakeracademic.com

Printed in the United States of America

Library of Congress Cataloging-in-Publication Data
Longman, Tremper.
    Old Testament commentary survey / Tremper Longman III. — Fifth edition.
        pages cm
    Includes bibliographical references and index.
    ISBN 978-0-8010-3991-1 (pbk. : alk. paper)
    1. Bible. O.T.—Commentaries—Bibliography. 2. Bible. O.T.—Commentaries—History and criticism. I. Title.
    Z7772.A1L64 2013
    [BS1151.52]
    016.2217—dc23   2012043064

13   14   15   16   17   18   19   7   6   5   4   3   2   1

In keeping with biblical principles of creation stewardship, Baker Publishing Group advocates the responsible use of our natural resources. As a member of the Green Press Initiative, our company uses recycled paper when possible. The text paper of this book is composed in part of post-consumer waste.

green press INITIATIVE

To
Bruce Fisk, Charles Farhadian, Maurice Lee, Bill Nelson,
Caryn Reeder, Helen Rhee, Curt Whiteman, Telford Work
Religious Studies Department, Westmont College

Contents

Preface to the Fifth Edition

As I said at the beginning of the fourth edition, time flies, and it did again. It's 2013 as I finish this fifth edition of the commentary survey that came out for the first time in 1991. The second edition appeared in 1995, the third in 2003, and the fourth in 2007. I had hoped to bring out this edition earlier, but it was not to be.

More commentaries have appeared, and so the selection of commentaries for purchase and use continues to grow larger, especially for some biblical books. It is therefore helpful to get a preliminary, though brief, assessment of such matters as intended audience, emphases, theological and methodological perspective, and quality.

As before, a number of excellent and good commentaries have been published in the past few years. There are also a number of mediocre ones but only the rare bad commentary. It's not easy writing commentaries, as I know now that I am the author of a number of them (appendix B). I continue to hope that future commentaries produced for use by Christian pastors in the church would include more reflection on how the Old Testament message is appropriated by the New Testament. I have more reason than ever to think my hope will be realized since I have developed as General Editor a new series for Zondervan that will have that as a main focus. Lord willing, by the next edition of this commentary series I will be evaluating the first volumes in that series.

Most of the popular commentaries are reviewed in these pages, but I have had to be selective. As I have done with each successive edition, I have omitted a number of commentaries that I reviewed in the previous edition to make room for new evaluations. If I have omitted one of your favorites, I apologize.

My hope is that this commentary survey will help students of the Bible choose those commentaries that are right for them, so they might more fully understand the Word of God.

Acknowledgments

When I began this project many years ago, I thought it would take a minimum amount of time and serve a limited readership. Many of my students had asked for my opinion on commentaries, but one of them, Eric Bauer, kept pestering me to compile a list and to make it available in our seminary bookstore. I figured I could devote a few minutes each day to writing a brief review of the best commentaries I know on certain biblical books. To make a long story short, Allan Fisher, director of publications at Baker, caught wind of my efforts and asked me to expand the list into a counterpart to Don Carson's *New Testament Commentary Survey*. I did not realize how much work was involved, but now that it is over, I would like to express my appreciation to both Eric and Allan for their encouragement to write this guide. The second edition was produced under the editorship of Jim Weaver. My good friend Jim Kinney edited the third, fourth, and now the fifth edition. Brian Bolger and his team always do an excellent job preparing the manuscript for publication.

I have now taught at Westmont College for fourteen years after eighteen years at Westminster Theological Seminary. I dedicated the fourth edition to my close friends and colleagues in the Old Testament Department there: Alan Groves, Peter Enns, Doug Green, and Mike Kelly. Mike and Doug are still there; Pete is teaching at Eastern

University. I am sad to report that Al died at an early age of melanoma soon after the publication of the fourth edition. We miss you, Al.

I would like to dedicate this edition to my present colleagues at Westmont College in the Religious Studies Department: Bill Nelson (OT), Bruce Fisk and Caryn Reeder (NT), Telford Work, Curt Whiteman, and Maurice Lee (Theology), Helen Rhee (Church History), and Charles Farhadian (World Religions). I could not ask for more collegial and intellectually stimulating people with whom to work.

Abbreviations

Bible Versions

NIV	New International Version	RSV	Revised Standard Version

Categories

L	Layperson
M	Minister
S	Scholar

Commentary Series

ACCS	Ancient Christian Commentary on Scripture	BCOTWP	Baker Commentary on the Old Testament: Wisdom and Psalms
AOTC	Apollos Old Testament Commentary	BSC	Bible Student's Commentary
AYBC	Anchor Yale Bible Commentary	BST	The Bible Speaks Today

BTCB	Brazos Theological Commentary on the Bible	NICOT	New International Commentary on the Old Testament
CBC	Cambridge Bible Commentary	NIVAC	New International Version Application Commentary
CC	Continental Commentaries	OTL	Old Testament Library
ComC	Communicator's Commentary	OTM	Old Testament Message
CsBC	Cornerstone Biblical Commentary	OTS	Old Testament Studies
DSB	The Daily Study Bible	PC	The Preacher's Commentary
EvBC	Everyman's Bible Commentary	REBC	Expositor's Bible Commentary: Revised Edition
FOTL	Forms of the Old Testament Literature	SHBC	Smyth and Helwys Bible Commentary
ICC	International Critical Commentary	TBC	Torch Bible Commentaries
Interp	Interpretation	THOTC	Two Horizons Old Testament Commentary
ITC	International Theological Commentary	TOTC	Tyndale Old Testament Commentaries
NAC	New American Commentary		
NCB	New Century Bible	UBCS	Understanding the Bible Commentary Series
NCBC	New Cambridge Bible Commentary	WBC	Word Biblical Commentary
NIB	New Interpreter's Bible	WEC	Wycliffe Exegetical Commentary
NIBCOT	New International Biblical Commentary on the Old Testament		

Introduction

Of making many books there is no end, and much study wearies the
body.

—Eccles. 12:12 (NIV)

While surveying the many commentaries listed in this guide, this
verse came to mind more than once. Sometimes it seemed as if a new
commentary appeared every week.

Upon more rational reflection, however, I found that there is a
dearth of commentaries on the Old Testament. This situation is not
simply because some commentaries are of little worth, but also because there are only a few commentaries on the books of the Old
Testament, although this situation is changing. Furthermore, no single
commentary, no matter how exhaustive, can provide all the information the reader might want and need. In addition, commentaries are
addressed to specialized audiences. A commentary written with the
needs of the layperson in mind often will not interest the scholar,
while one written for a scholarly audience is often of no use to the
layperson. Ministers have enough training to be interested in answers
to technical questions but also want help in making the text relevant
to the people in their congregation.

Who Should Read This Guide?

There are many commentaries available. As a specialist in Old Testament, I do not think I have been asked any question more frequently than "What's the best commentary on . . . ?"

This guide is for anyone, layperson or minister, who desires to buy a commentary. It lists a number of works available for each book of the Old Testament, briefly summarizes their emphases and viewpoints, and evaluates them. This guide will be especially helpful to seminary students beginning to build the reference library that will be crucial to their preaching and teaching ministries.

Evaluation

Some might disagree with me in the value I assign to individual commentaries. It is accordingly of some interest to know what I value in a commentary and the perspective from which I write.

I represent an evangelical approach to the Old Testament and, accordingly, give high marks to good commentaries that come from a similar perspective. However, it is important to emphasize the adjective *good*. I can appreciate and learn from writers who write from a perspective different than my own, but I am particularly hard on shallow or incompetent commentaries that come from the perspective I advocate.

I evaluate commentaries on a 1-to-5 scale. One or two stars indicate that the commentary is inferior or deficient, and I discourage its purchase. Four or five stars is a high mark. Three, obviously, means a commentary is good but not great. I also use half stars in order to refine the system of evaluation. Please note that my own commentaries are unrated. For a separate listing of my commentaries, see appendix B.

I also indicate who would most benefit from the commentary under consideration. There are three categories: L(ayperson); M(inister) (seminary students should consider themselves in this category); and S(cholar). I provide page counts for each volume, with small roman numerals indicating the pages of introductory material.

For a similar guide to the New Testament, please consult D. A. Carson, *New Testament Commentary Survey*, 7th ed. (Baker Academic, forthcoming).

The Use and Abuse of Commentaries

There is a right way and a wrong way to use a commentary. Actually, there are two wrong ways. The first is to ignore completely the use of commentaries. Some people do not consult commentaries because they believe that, since all Christians are equal as they approach the Scriptures, scholars have no privileged insight into the biblical text. The second error is to become overly dependent on commentaries. "These people have devoted their whole lives to the study of the Bible. How can my opinion measure up to theirs?"

Those holding the first position are wrong because they forget that God gives different gifts to different people in the church. Not all people are equally adept at understanding the Bible and teaching it to others (1 Cor. 12:12–31). Those holding the second position err in the opposite direction. They forget that God has given believers the Spirit by which they can discern spiritual things (1 Cor. 2:14–16).

The right way to use a commentary is as a help. We should first study a passage without reference to any helps. Only after coming to an initial understanding of the passage should we consult commentaries.

Neither should we let commentaries bully us. Many times they will be of great help, but sometimes the reader will be right and the commentaries will be wrong.

One-Volume
Commentaries

One-volume commentaries are commentaries on the whole Bible bound in one volume. They generally have between 1,000 and 1,500 pages. While their comments on individual books are too short to provide insight into a text, such volumes are handy to have around for a quick orientation to a book or passage of Scripture. They are relatively inexpensive and are good choices for laypeople who do not want to invest in a series. There are also some excellent study Bibles available that basically function as one-volume commentaries. The three best out there right now are the *NIV Study Bible*, the *NLT Study Bible*, and the *ESV Study Bible*.

Berlin, A., and M. Brettler, eds. *The Jewish Study Bible*. Oxford, 2003. 2181 pp.

This study Bible is of great interest not just to Jewish but also to Christian readers of the Bible. The editors and contributors are all top-flight scholars who know how to write to a general audience. As the introduction points out, there is not one single Jewish interpretive approach to the text, and most of the contributors represent a moderate critical approach to the text, but they are also conversant with and discuss earlier Jewish interpretive approaches to the text. LM★★★↲

Burge, G. M., and A. E. Hill, eds. *The Baker Illustrated Bible Commentary.* Baker Books, 2012. 1648 pp.

This commentary is the most up-to-date and best available, and there are pictures! For reasons of disclosure, I did the Micah commentary, but the contributors are generally very good, including some well-known names like Mark Boda, Roy Gane, Victor Hamilton, Andrew Hill, Robert Holmstedt, Walter Kaiser, Elmer Martens, Elaine Phillips, Richard Schultz, Gary Smith, and Willem VanGemeren (not to mention the New Testament contributors). LM★★★★★

Carson, D. A., R. T. France, J. A. Motyer, and G. J. Wenham, eds. *New Bible Commentary: Twenty-First Century Edition.* InterVarsity, 1994. 1455 pp.

This volume is a thorough revision of the earlier *New Bible Commentary Revised*. It brings the latter up-to-date through the work of many leading Old and New Testament scholars. The introductory and general articles are helpful and well written. LM★★★★★

Dunn, J. D. G., and J. Rogerson, eds. *Eerdmans Commentary on the Bible.* Eerdmans, 2000. 1649 pp.

Utilizing the talents of scholars representing a broad theological spectrum, the Eerdmans commentary provides readers with a concise, stimulating, sometimes provocative reading of the biblical text. LM★★★★

Walton, J. H., V. H. Matthews, and M. W. Chavalas. *The IVP Bible Background Commentary: Old Testament.* InterVarsity, 2000. 832 pp.

This easy-to-use reference book concentrates on the ancient Near Eastern background that otherwise is so difficult for the modern lay reader but that is also incredibly illuminating. LM★★★★★

Commentary
Sets and Series

Publishers have found that commentaries sell best in a set. There are a number of commentary sets currently in production. The following list serves two purposes. First, it describes more fully and evaluates those sets that are written by one or two authors. Second, it describes the method of other sets by multiple authors. The individual volumes found in this second group are described and evaluated in the following section, which proceeds book by book through the Bible. It should be noted that sets with a number of different authors often vary in quality. It is often best to choose among commentaries rather than committing oneself to a single set of commentaries. The asterisks indicate those series whose individual volumes I try to include consistently.

*Anchor Yale Bible Commentaries (AYBC). Ed. D. N. Freedman. Doubleday. Reprinted by Yale University Press.

The Anchor Yale Bible Commentaries is an indispensable tool for scholars and certain ministers, but it often fails in its attempt to communicate with laypersons. It usually emphasizes philology, historical background, and text, rather than theology. The volumes range in quality from excellent to horrible. MS★★★

Ancient Christian Commentary on Scripture: Old Testament (ACCS). Ed. T. C. Oden. InterVarsity.

In the past ten or fifteen years, early interpretation has received renewed interest especially from those of us who value the theological significance of the biblical passages. These volumes, produced by historical theologians and church historians, present excerpts from early interpretations of a text to give the flavor of interpretive tendencies of the past for readers who do not have the time to extensively research the voluminous primary material. MS★★★★★

*Apollos Old Testament Commentary (AOTC). Ed. D. W. Baker and G. J. Wenham. InterVarsity.

The Apollos commentary now has five contributions (Leviticus, Deuteronomy, Joshua, Samuel, and Daniel), and these hold much promise for the future. The commentaries are clearly written and conversant with the best scholarship. The purpose of the series is to keep "one foot firmly planted in the universe of the original text and the other in that of the target audience." MS★★★★★

*Baker Commentary on the Old Testament: Wisdom and Psalms (BCOTWP). Ed. T. Longman III. Baker Academic.

Delimiting this series to Psalms and Wisdom allows concentration on distinctive elements of those genres. The focus is on theological message. As of 2012 and the publication of my Job commentary, the series is now complete. LM★★★★★

Berit Olam. Ed. D. W. Cotter. Michael Glazier.

This series is just under way and provides a focus on the literary analysis of the books. This means different things to the contributors, as may be seen by comparing J. T. Walsh's close reading of 1 Kings with D. Jobling's postmodern analysis of 1 Samuel. MS★★★

*The Bible Speaks Today (BST). Ed. J. A. Motyer (Old Testament), J. Stott (New Testament), and D. Tidball (the new BST Bible Themes). InterVarsity.

The purpose of this set is to write on the biblical text in a way that engages the reader. In other words, its volumes can be read cover to cover; they are not simply reference tools. The series is readable, accurate, and relevant. LM★★★★

*Brazos Theological Commentary on the Bible (BTCB). Ed. R. R. Reno. Brazos.

As the title to the series implies, these volumes take a decidedly theological approach to the text. Written by theologians and propelled by a distaste for the historical-critical (and seemingly for a historical-grammatical) method, sometimes the commentaries seem to have little contact with the text itself, though some volumes are very helpful. MS★★★

Calvin's Commentaries. 22 vols. Reprint, Baker.

These commentaries find their origin in Calvin's sermons, but they are learned and theologically insightful. It is no wonder that Calvin is called the "prince of expositors." Calvin does comment on language occasionally, but one will have to consult a more recent commentary because of discoveries in the Hebrew language. He does not cover the whole Old Testament; there are no volumes for Judges through Job. The five-volume commentary on Psalms is wonderful. Unfortunately, Calvin harmonizes Exodus to Deuteronomy. LMS★★★★★

Cambridge Bible Commentary (CBC). Ed. P. R. Ackroyd, A. R. C. Leaney, and J. W. Packer. Cambridge University Press.

This series is composed of short and readable commentaries on all the books of the Old Testament and the Apocrypha. They intend to bring the fruits of contemporary scholarship to educated laypersons. The volumes also intend to explicate the New English Bible, which is the base of the commentary. They concentrate on both historical and theological issues. A selection of volumes includes R. E. Clements on Exodus; P. R. Ackroyd on Samuel; R. J. Coggins on Chronicles; J. D. W. Watts on the Minor Prophets; and R. N. Whybray on Proverbs. LM★★★

Concordia Commentary (ConC). Concordia Publishing House.

The Concordia Commentary reflects a conservative Lutheran perspective. Though the Lutheran perspective comes through loud and clear, the reader does not have to be Lutheran to benefit from the often-insightful exegesis. The Old Testament volumes have an emphasis on how the text "promotes Christ," which should prove helpful to ministers who want to preach Christ from the Old Testament. LM★★★★

Continental Commentaries (CC). Augsburg/Fortress.

This series translates into English leading German commentaries from various series. They are critical commentaries that on occasion are fairly technical, though not to the level of Hermeneia. Though technical and critical, the careful reader can benefit greatly from the number of significant theological insights on the various books. Not many volumes have yet appeared, and they are not in a rush, it appears, to get them out. MS★★★

Cornerstone Biblical Commentary (CsBC). Ed. P. W. Comfort. Tyndale.

This new series is based on the New Living Translation and seeks to exposit the text. The text is interpreted section by section, and each section is followed by more specific exegetical notes. The series is now complete and is a very helpful midsize commentary. LM★★★★

The Daily Study Bible (DSB). 24 vols. Ed. J. C. L. Gibson. Westminster John Knox.

The DSB is the Old Testament counterpart to Barclay's New Testament commentaries. The name derives from the fact that the commentators have divided the text (RSV) into portions that can be read in a single day's devotional. The commentary is directed toward the layperson and encourages an expositional and theological reading of the text. LM★★★★

Expositor's Bible Commentary: Revised Edition (REBC). Ed. D. Garland and T. Longman III. Zondervan.

This is a revised edition of the popular commentary series that originally was edited by Frank Gaebelein but now is edited by David Garland and yours truly. Each volume comments on more than one book (except *Psalms* by VanGemeren, which is a stand-alone). About 40 percent of the contributions are updates and revisions by authors who produced the first edition in the late seventies and eighties, but about 60 percent are totally new works. As of 2012, the series is now complete. LM★★★★✔

*Forms of the Old Testament Literature (FOTL). Ed. R. Knierim and G. M. Tucker. Eerdmans.

When completed, this series will have twenty-four volumes. The title of the series indicates its focus on a form-critical approach to the text. Judged in the light of their purpose, these are excellent commentaries. Scholars will find these books invaluable. S★★★★

*Hermeneia. Ed. F. M. Cross et al. Fortress/SCM.

A number of the volumes in this series are translations of original German works, although there are some English contributions. The quality of the series is high. It intends to deliver the best of historical and critical scholarship, and it usually succeeds. There are some classic works in this series. S★★★★★

International Critical Commentary (ICC). T&T Clark.

These are highly technical studies of philology and text. They are best used by specialists and retain their value in spite of their age. A new series is presently being written. S★★★

International Theological Commentary (ITC). Handsel.

This is a series of short commentaries written from a third-world perspective. The purpose is both to shake off some of the assumptions of Western readers and to connect the text with contemporary issues. It often provides interesting insight into the Bible. At other times, however, these volumes are scarcely distinguishable from traditional commentaries. LM★★

*Interpretation (Interp). Ed. J. L. Mays. Westminster John Knox.

This series bridges the gap between scholarly investigation and contemporary relevance. Moderately critical, the series is readable and interesting. LM★★★★

*JPS Torah Commentary. Ed. N. M. Sarna. Jewish Publication Society.

The series, as the title indicates, will cover only the first five books of the Hebrew Bible. The commentary prints the Hebrew text and gives copious comments on philology, history of research (with very interesting comments from rabbinic material), and theology. The content and the production of the volumes are first-rate. MS★★★★★

Keil-Delitzsch. 10 vols. Eerdmans.

C. F. Keil and F. Delitzsch were orthodox Lutheran Old Testament scholars from Germany in the latter half of the nineteenth century. Their expositions, although dated, are solid and competent. They often give helpful theological commentary as well. This set is fairly inexpensive and makes a good backbone to a minister's library. LM★★★★

Knox Preaching Guides. Ed. J. H. Hayes. Westminster John Knox.

These short paperbacks offer assistance to ministers as they prepare to preach. They include a number of notable contributors, such as W. Brueggemann, J. J. Collins, W. Roth, E. Achtemeier, and J. G. Gammie, and are moderately critical for the most part. M★★★

Layman's Bible Commentary. Westminster John Knox.

Short, concise commentaries written for the layperson by critical scholars of the past generation. LM★★

Leupold's Commentaries. Baker.

Leupold was a conservative Lutheran who wrote on many Old Testament books (Genesis, Psalms, Ecclesiastes, Isaiah, Daniel, and Zechariah). Leupold's work has value, but he tends to write more like a systematic theologian than a biblical exegete. LM★★

*The Minor Prophets. Ed. T. McComiskey. Baker.

In most series, the Minor Prophets are given short shrift. This series intends to give the Minor Prophets their due. While not every contribution is the best on its particular book, this is the best anthology of commentaries on the Minor Prophets available. MS★★★★★

*New American Commentary (NAC). Ed. E. Ray Clendenen. Broadman.

This relatively new series is making a strong entry into the field of commentaries. Based on the NIV text, it is an expository commentary with an emphasis on the theological message of the Bible as a whole. It adopts a clear evangelical approach to the text. Most of the volumes in the series have appeared and are highly competent, and some are outstanding (see Block on Judges and Ruth for instance). MS★★★✔

*New Century Bible (NCB). Ed. R. E. Clements (Old Testament). Sheffield.

The New Century Bible is a predominantly British project based on the RSV. Many of the volumes seem restricted by the format. As a series, it is weak. There are, however, some very fine volumes. The volumes range from moderately critical to heavily critical. LM★★

*New International Biblical Commentary on the Old Testament (NIBCOT). Ed. R. L. Hubbard Jr. and R. Johnston. Hendrickson/Paternoster.

See under Understanding the Bible Commentary Series.

*New International Commentary on the Old Testament (NICOT). Ed. R. L. Hubbard Jr. Eerdmans.

This series was originally begun in the 1950s under E. J. Young's editorship but was stalled after the editor produced his three-volume Isaiah commentary. Young's commentary has since been removed. The series is evangelical and scholarly but written in a way that laypeople can understand. Technical issues as well as theological commentary are found in these commentaries. R. Hubbard has taken over since the death of R. K. Harrison. MS★★★★

*New International Version Application Commentary (NIVAC). Ed. A. Dearman, R. L. Hubbard Jr., T. Longman III, and J. H. Walton. Zondervan/Hodder & Stoughton.

NIVAC comments on each unit under three topics: original meaning, bridging contexts, and contemporary significance. Excellent for the preacher. LM★★★★★

New Interpreter's Bible (NIB). Ed. L. E. Keck et al. Abingdon.

This series replaces the long-honored original *Interpreter's Bible* that was produced in the 1950s. The format is a cross between a set and individual book commentaries. The Old Testament is covered in six volumes. The commentary has two sections: a more technical exegetical section and an expository section. A diversity of theological viewpoints is represented, but whether evangelical or not, all the contributors seem committed to the theological authority of the text. LM★★★

*Old Testament Library (OTL). Ed. P. R. Ackroyd et al. Westminster John Knox/SCM.

This is a distinguished collection of commentaries written in the critical tradition. Many, but not all, are translations of earlier German works. OTL includes, besides the commentaries, Eichrodt's *Theology*, Beyerlin's study of related ancient Near Eastern texts, and Soggin's history. MS★★★

Old Testament Message (OTM). Ed. C. Stuhlmueller and M. McNamara. Michael Glazier.

OTM is planned to be a twenty-three-volume set, geared for laypeople. While each volume is written by a Catholic scholar, it is hoped by the editors that the appeal will be much broader. The method is moderately critical with a premium on clarity, theology, and relevance. LM★★★

The Preacher's Commentary (PC). Nelson.

First known as the Communicator's Commentary and then as Mastering the Old Testament, Thomas Nelson now publishes it as the Preacher's Commentary. This energetic commentary is directed toward pastors and other Christian leaders who teach. For the most part, the volumes meet their intended goal and are backed by solid scholarship. The volumes are very readable. LM★★★

Smyth and Helwys Bible Commentary (SHBC). Smyth and Helwys.

SHBC is a very user-friendly commentary series. It even comes with a CD-ROM. The contributions so far come from scholars who can be described as moderately critical and theologically sensitive. The series has some excellent contributions (Brueggemann on Kings; Fretheim on Jeremiah) and some that are not helpful at all (Biddle on Deuteronomy). The biggest problem with this series is the price of the volumes. LM★★

Torch Bible Commentaries (TBC). Ed. J. Marsh, A. Richardson, and R. G. Smith. SCM.

This series is very similar in intent, scope, and approach to the Cambridge Bible Commentaries. The contributors were asked to make the results of modern scholarship accessible to educated laypeople within the church. Two notable contributions include J. H. Eaton on Psalms and C. R. North on Isaiah 40–55. The commentary is based on the Authorized Version. LM★★★

Two Horizons Old Testament Commentaries (THOTC). Eerdmans.

Like the Brazos series (see above), this series intends to feed the interest in theological exegesis, but this series, in my opinion, does a much better job of it. Written primarily by biblical scholars, there is rich and illuminating interest in the biblical text itself. The one exception is the Joshua volume which was half written by a theologian, and that half is problematic. The first half of each volume is an exposition of the text, and the second half a lengthy and interesting theological reflection. MS★★★★↗

*Tyndale Old Testament Commentaries (TOTC). Ed. D. J. Wiseman. InterVarsity.

These commentaries are authored by respected English, South African, Australian, Irish, and American evangelical scholars. They are in the main directed toward a nonspecialist audience. They emphasize exegesis. They are brief, but usually informative. The second generation TOTC commentaries are beginning to appear with David Firth as main editor and me as consulting editor. Over the next ten or so years new volumes will appear for every book. The first volume on Deuteronomy by Woods has been published and is reviewed in this volume. LM★★★

*Understanding the Bible Commentary Series (UBCS). Ed. R. L. Hubbard Jr. and R. Johnston. Baker Books.

This series is committed to what the editors call "believing criticism," which tries to navigate between a kind of criticism that never gets to the meaning of the final form of the text and a theological dogmatism. Previously published as New International Biblical Commentary on the Old Testament (NIBCOT). LM★★★★

*Word Biblical Commentary (WBC). Ed. J. D. W. Watts (Old Testament). Nelson/Paternoster.

These commentaries are written by evangelicals identified in the preface as those committed "to Scripture as divine revelation, and to the truth and power of the Christian gospel." This definition allows for the wide-ranging approaches to the Bible found in the series. Not everyone will be satisfied that a given commentary is evangelical in its theological orientation, although most of the volumes clearly are. These commentaries are very learned and provide their own translation with philological, textual, and literary notes. Theological message is also treated, but, with a few exceptions, these theological comments rarely bridge the gap to the New Testament. MS★★★★

Zondervan Illustrated Bible Backgrounds Commentary. Ed. J. H. Walton. Zondervan.

This wonderful resource (for reasons of disclosure, I should mention that I did Proverbs) speaks exclusively about the cultural background of the various Old Testament books. Beautifully illustrated, the commentary comes in five volumes. The contributors are experts in the Old Testament and the ancient Near East and are all evangelicals. LM★★★★★

Individual Commentaries

GENESIS

Aalders, G. C. *Genesis*. 2 vols. BSC. Zondervan, 1981. 311 pp. and 228 pp.

This is an English translation of a commentary originally published in Dutch in 1949. Although somewhat dated, Aalders's work retains its value as a theological commentary. Writing from within the Reformed tradition, Aalders shows great exegetical skill and theological insight. MS★↗

Atkinson, D. *The Message of Genesis 1–11: The Dawn of Creation*. BST. InterVarsity, 1990. 190 pp.

A brief, expository, and devotional reading of the first part of the book of Genesis. Atkinson is insightful and knowledgeable. LM★↗

Baldwin, J. G. *The Message of Genesis 12–50: From Abraham to Joseph*. BST. InterVarsity, 1986. 224 pp.

Baldwin writes in a popular style, yet there is no doubt that considerable scholarly research stands behind her commentary. Her approach to Genesis 12–50 is traditional, yet not stodgy. LM★★★

Briscoe, S. *Genesis*. ComC. Word, 1987. 414 pp.

Briscoe does a good job navigating the difficult interpretive issues of Genesis. Not that he is always right, but he exercises fairly sensible judgment. The volume, in keeping with the purpose of the commentary, is sermonic and anecdotal, not exegetical or biblical-theological. However, what it does, it does well. LM★★ɟ

Brueggemann, W. *Genesis*. Interp. Westminster John Knox, 1982. viii/384 pp.

Brueggemann, although a moderately critical scholar, is always stimulating and insightful. His commentary concentrates on the final form of the text and focuses principally on the theology of the book. LM★★★★

Cassuto, U. *From Adam to Abraham: A Commentary on the Book of Genesis*. Trans. I. Abrahams. 2 vols. Magnes, 1964. xviii/323 pp. and xiv/386 pp.

This is a solid commentary on the first eleven chapters of Genesis. Cassuto, a conservative Jewish writer, died unexpectedly before the book was completed. He was a brilliant philologist and literary scholar. He, interestingly, goes against the scholarly tide and rejects the Documentary Hypothesis. S★★★

Coats, G. W. *Genesis with an Introduction to Narrative Literature*. FOTL. Eerdmans, 1983. xiii/322 pp.

Definitely one of the best volumes in the series thus far, this commentary nonetheless is difficult to wade through due to its focus on form-critical issues. Coats is most helpful when he deals with narrative issues from a literary standpoint. He is least helpful when he spends time analyzing the sources of the narrative rather than concentrating on the final form of the text. S★★★

Gibson, J. C. L. *Genesis*. 2 vols. DSB. Westminster John Knox, 1981. ix/214 pp. and 322 pp.

In keeping with the nature of the series, Gibson writes in a popular vein. He helpfully opens up the text for lay understanding, showing the relevance of Genesis for the Christian. He is less helpful when he describes the composition of the book along the lines of older source criticism. LM★★★

Gowan, D. E. *Genesis 1–11*. ITC. Handsel, 1988. ix/125 pp.

A short theological study of the first eleven chapters of the Bible. While there is considerable theological reflection, the book also displays a fair share of typical critical assumptions. Gowan's treatment of the relationship between the theology and history of Genesis is quite superficial and will not satisfy many. While many of the commentaries in this series come from a third-world perspective, this one does not. It also fails to interact with contemporary social and political issues to the extent of many of the other volumes. LM★★

Hamilton, V. P. *The Book of Genesis*. 2 vols. NICOT. Eerdmans, 1990, 1995. 522 pp. and 774 pp.

Hamilton does an excellent job interpreting the text in a positive way as well as handling the difficult questions of the book (creation story, history of patriarchs, religion of patriarchs). Between Wenham and Hamilton, Genesis is well covered. MS★★★★✔

Hartley, J. E. *Genesis*. UBCS. Baker Books, 2000. xvii/393 pp.

I cannot always agree with Hartley's analysis of the structure of the book of Genesis or with his analysis of sections of it as a palistrophe (the arrangement of material in a V-shaped pattern, also known as chiasm), but Hartley nonetheless offers a clear and straightforward analysis of the book of Genesis. The depth of exposition is constrained by the series. His arguments in favor of Mosaic involvement in the production of the book and also in favor of the patriarchal narratives is refreshing. LM★★★★

Kidner, D. *Genesis.* TOTC. InterVarsity, 1967. 224 pp.

This is an excellent commentary within the parameters of the series. Since it is so brief, it cannot hope to fully comment on the text. It is noticeably lacking (by design) substantial philological notes. It is written from a solidly conservative standpoint. This is a good starter commentary for the layperson. LM★★★

Maher, M. *Genesis.* OTM. Michael Glazier, 1982. 279 pp.

The volume may have some value in its theological commentary. It presents the rather naive critical view that Genesis is a "statement of religious truths" rather than history. Maher accepts the now dated Documentary Hypothesis, although he notes challenges to it in passing. LM★★

Mathews, K. A. *Genesis 1–11:26.* NAC. Broadman, 1996. *Genesis 11:27–50:26.* NAC. Broadman, 2005. 526 pp. and 960 pp.

Mathews has produced an excellent study of the primeval history with an emphasis on the text as literature and theology. He does not shrink from the difficult historical and philological issues either. He navigates well the relationship between these chapters and ancient Near Eastern literature. Mathews continues his careful and helpful work in the second volume. Among other things, he interacts extensively with the modern discussion of issues of historicity. LM★★★★✦

McKeown, J. *Genesis.* Two Horizons. Eerdmans, 2008. ix/398 pp.

After a short commentary emphasizing the theological message of the book of Genesis, McKeown then gives a series of thematic essays on the book beginning with the "main unifying themes" (descendants, blessing, land), as well as the book's "key theological teaching" (including the doctrine of creation, the fall, the image of God, and more), "Genesis and theology today" (Genesis and science, mission, ecology, etc.), and "biblical theology," which places the book in the context of the rest of the canon. Interesting and competent. LM★★★★✦

Reno, R. R. *Genesis*. BTCB. Brazos, 2010. 304 pp.

Written by a theologian from a theologian's point of view, there is little of what a biblical scholar might call exegesis here. He treats at length sporadic verses. As he puts it, "No single rule or principle guides my judgments about what makes for a telling verse, and as a result I do not follow a consistent method or pattern of exegesis" (21). Not recommended except perhaps after reading some of the better truly exegetical commentaries. LM★★

Ross, A. P. *Creation and Blessing: A Guide to the Study and Exposition of Genesis*. Baker, 1988. 744 pp.

The book opens with a short introduction to the whole book, stating the author's approach to Genesis. Ross presents an evangelical alternative to the documentary approach. The bulk of his treatment, however, is more like a running exposition with an emphasis on theology. As such it is often insightful and helpful. A good book, especially for pastors preaching through the book of Genesis. LM★★★✦

Sailhamer, J. *Genesis*. REBC 1. Zondervan, 2008. Pp. 21–332.

Sailhamer is known for his "compositional analysis," in which he analyzes various connections using lexical and thematic data to show connections between various sections of the book and with the rest of the Old Testament. Sometimes this is illuminating, but most often it seems stretched. LM★★★

Sarna, N. M. *Understanding Genesis: The Heritage of Biblical Israel*. Schocken, 1966. 245 pp.

This readable commentary is written from a pious Jewish perspective that takes into account a moderate historical-critical approach and attempts to make Genesis meaningful and relevant to an educated lay audience. Sarna believes that God can work through four sources (JEDP) as well as a unified book and further argues that historical criticism supports rather than denies faith. Short, but readable, with an emphasis on interpretation and comparative studies. MS★★★

Sarna, N. M. *Genesis.* JPS Torah Commentary. Jewish Publication Society, 1989. xxi/414 pp.

This commentary is considerably more academic in approach than the one published in 1966. It studies the text in a verse-by-verse, virtually word-by-word, manner. Although Sarna recognizes the composite nature of Genesis, he treats the book as a whole in the commentary. His emphasis, although he deals with other aspects of the text, is on Near Eastern background and Jewish tradition. MS★★★★

Scullion, J. J. *Genesis: A Commentary for Students, Teachers, and Preachers.* OTS. Liturgical/Michael Glazier, 1992. xviii/366 pp.

This commentary, published right after Scullion's death, is a strong, traditionally critical approach to the book. Not that the author lacks his own distinctive approach, but he fails to take into account important recent developments in literary approaches and also recent insights from source criticism. Nonetheless, he is strong on the history of research up to the most recent developments and also on ancient Near Eastern background. M★★★

Skinner, J. *A Critical and Exegetical Commentary on Genesis.* ICC. T&T Clark, 1910. lxvi/552 pp.

This volume represents the best of turn-of-the-century critical thought. Skinner does a detailed source analysis of the book along the lines of the Documentary Hypothesis. This is an extremely detailed commentary. Helpful grammatical information may be found here. The book is in small print, however, and is often hard to read. Not recommended for the layperson or pastor. S★

Speiser, E. A. *Genesis.* AYBC. Yale University Press, 1964. lxxiv/379 pp.

Speiser takes a fairly classical, critical approach to the book of Genesis in the delineation of sources. The introduction separates P, J, and E sources (the order in which they appear in the book) and then discusses the residue. Speiser is of some help in matters of language, since he was one of the preeminent Semitic linguists of his day. This commentary is a classic and probably is a must-buy for the scholar, but of little use to anyone else. S★

von Rad, G. *Genesis*. OTL. Westminster John Knox/SCM, 1972. 440 pp.

An insightful, but critical, commentary on Genesis. Von Rad is sensitive to theology and literature. He is not known for his work on the Hebrew language. He argues for the Hexateuch and delineates sources. S★★★

Waltke, B. K., and C. J. Fredricks. *Genesis*. Zondervan, 2001. 656 pp.

This commentary is not in a series but is well worth tracking down and adding to a reference library. Waltke is the dean of evangelical biblical scholars, and this commentary is exegetically insightful and theologically rich. LM★★★★★

Walton, J. H. *Genesis*. NIVAC. Zondervan/Hodder & Stoughton, 2001. 752 pp.

Walton's commentary is stimulating and well written. He navigates the difficult issues of the book well. Unfortunately, he rarely comments on the relationship between Genesis and the New Testament. LM★★★★

Wenham, G. J. *Genesis 1–15*. WBC. Nelson/Paternoster, 1987. *Genesis 16–50*. WBC. Nelson/Paternoster, 1994. liii/353 pp. and 555 pp.

Wenham is one of the finest evangelical commentators today. His commentary on Genesis shows his high level of scholarship and his exegetical sensitivity. He represents a conservative approach to Genesis, but he does not completely reject source theory. LM★★★✓

Westermann, C. *Genesis*. 3 vols. CC. Fortress/SPCK, 1984–86. xii/636 pp., 604 pp., and 269 pp.

These three volumes were originally published in German between 1974 and 1982. This commentary is a fully conceived approach that takes into account text, form, setting, interpretation, purpose, and thrust. It also provides excellent bibliographies for each section and synthesizes previous research. It claims to be the first major commentary on Genesis in decades and is from a moderately critical stance. MS★★★

Youngblood, R. *The Book of Genesis: An Introductory Commentary*. Baker, 1991. 295 pp.

This volume is a reworking of two volumes that Youngblood published in 1976 and 1980. The focus is on the book's teaching, not on philology or form. The introduction, which deals with questions of authorship and date, among other issues, is adequate for the volume, which is directed toward laypeople. The writing style is engaging and clear. LM★★★

EXODUS

Bruckner, J. *Exodus*. UBCS. Baker Books, 2008. ix/348 pp.

An intelligent, nuanced, relatively brief treatment of the book of Exodus. Bruckner is especially adept at bringing out the theological significance of the book. LM★★★★✔

Burns, R. J. *Exodus, Leviticus, Numbers*. OTM. Michael Glazier, 1983. 298 pp.

The author takes a traditional literary-critical approach to these three pentateuchal books. She asserts that Exodus "must be read as a religious creed and not as a historical chronicle" (19). She does not treat every chapter of all three books, and Leviticus and Numbers get less attention than Exodus. LM★

Cassuto, U. *Commentary on the Book of Exodus.* Trans. I. Abrahams. Magnes, 1967. xvi/509 pp.

Cassuto rejects the Documentary Hypothesis and explains the existing text. He is sensitive to the literary artistry of Exodus and brilliant in his philological analysis. See also comments under his commentary on Genesis. S★★★

Childs, B. S. *The Book of Exodus.* OTL. Westminster John Knox/ SCM, 1974. xxv/659 pp.

This is one of the best commentaries on Exodus. Childs divides his commentary into different sections, including textual criticism and philology, critical methods, Old Testament context, New Testament context, and history of interpretation. Although representing a critical perspective, this volume is valuable to evangelical ministers. MS★★★★

Coats, G. W. *Exodus 1–18.* FOTL. Eerdmans, 1999. xiv/178 pp.

The preface explains the difficult journey that this volume had to reach publication and this in large part explains why this book is not even close to being up to the standard of the rest of the series. S★

Cole, R. A. *Exodus.* TOTC. InterVarsity, 1973. 239 pp.

As is the case with all the volumes in this series, this is a book with all the inherent disadvantages of a short commentary. There is not much of general introduction or interaction with source criticism, but there is an excellent theological introduction. LM★★

Durham, J. I. *Exodus.* WBC. Nelson/Paternoster, 1987. xxxiv/516 pp.

The strength of this commentary is its focus on the theology of the text. Its weakness is its casual attitude toward the historicity of Exodus. Durham identifies the heart of the book's message as the presence of God with God's people. MS★★★★

Ellison, H. L. *Exodus.* DSB. Westminster John Knox, 1982. 203 pp.

Ellison does a good job explaining the text to the modern lay reader. He is insightful, but the commentary is too brief. The introduction is short, even for the series, and makes only passing reference to the critical problems of history. Ellison emphasizes theology and is committed to a New Testament approach after studying the text in its Old Testament context. LM★★

Enns, P. *Exodus.* NIVAC. Zondervan/Hodder & Stoughton, 2000. 448 pp.

Enns has produced an incredibly insightful theological study of the book. He also deals well with the important historical issues, but not from a technical standpoint. This commentary is ideal for those preaching on Exodus, because he so thoughtfully explores the book's trajectory toward the New Testament gospel. LM★★★★★

Fretheim, T. E. *Exodus.* Interp. Westminster John Knox, 1990. xii/321 pp.

This very readable volume is stimulating in discussing the theological message of the book of Exodus. Fretheim might be described as a moderate critic who concentrates on the final form of the text. This volume is not particularly helpful on the more technical aspects of the book. LM★★★★

Gispen, W. H. *Exodus.* BSC. Zondervan, 1982. 335 pp.

Gispen's work was originally published in Dutch in 1951. It is full of helpful exegetical and theological insights from a Reformed perspective. MS★★★

Hamilton, V. P. *Exodus: An Exegetical Commentary.* Baker Academic, 2011. xxix/721 pp.

As the subtitle indicates, this excellent commentary by an able interpreter focuses on exegesis and thus provides its own translations with notes as well as a good treatment of the text's meaning without much further theological or canonical reflection. LM★★★★

Kaiser, W. C., Jr. *Exodus*. REBC 1. Zondervan, 2008. Pp. 333–561.

A good, basic commentary, but a tad dated since Kaiser did not do much updating from the earlier edition of the commentary published in 1990. LM★★

Meyers, C. L. *Exodus*. NCBC. Cambridge, 2005. xiii/309 pp.

This commentary is interesting to read cover to cover. It is insightful in terms of the original meaning of the text, though conservative readers will not agree with her assessment of the historicity of Exodus. It is very winsomely written. LM★★★★

Noth, M. *Exodus*. Trans. J. Bowden. OTL. Westminster John Knox/SCM, 1962. 283 pp.

Noth is one of the most important German critical scholars of the previous century. He concentrates on historical and literary issues from a critical perspective. This is an important piece of scholarship but will not help the pastor or layperson. S★★★

Propp, W. H. C. *Exodus 1–18*. AYBC. Yale University Press, 1998. *Exodus 19–40*. AYBC. Yale University Press, 2006. xl/680 pp. and xxx/865 pp.

Propp's commentary has some unique features compared to other volumes in the series. For one thing, each section begins with comments on text, source, and redaction criticism. Also, contrary to the practice of most biblical scholars, Propp marks a speculative remark as speculation (other scholars will judge that some of his unmarked comments are equally speculative!). His opening translation is quite literal, even awkwardly so. Many readers will find these features a bit confusing and off-putting, but there are some excellent insights into the text. MS★★↲

Sarna, N. M. *Exodus*. JPS Torah Commentary. Jewish Publication Society, 1991. 304 pp.

Sarna is one of the masters of commentary-writing on the Torah. This volume is noticeably shorter than the others in the series and lacks their vitality. Nonetheless, the serious student should consult it. MS★★★

Stuart, D. *Exodus*. NAC. Broadman, 2006. 827 pp.

A well-written exposition of the book from an evangelical perspective. One wishes for a more extensive reflection on the relationship between the theology of Exodus with the New Testament, but still many important insights. LM★★★↲

LEVITICUS

Bailey, L. R. *Leviticus and Numbers*. SHBC. Smyth and Helwys, 2005. 648 pp.

An accessible but somewhat unremarkable commentary. When it is remarkable, it is sometimes objectionable, as in the introduction, which suggests that Christians, including some New Testament authors, rejected the "Levitical way of life" out of passionate anti-Semitism. Better to buy Milgrom as an academic commentary and Gane to bridge the gap between the ancient text and the modern world. LM★↲

Balentine, S. E. *Leviticus*. Interp. Westminster John Knox, 2002. xv/220 pp.

Balentine tries to understand and appreciate the significance of the ritual law of Leviticus, a noble goal indeed. He often provides help and insight, but his commentary is a bit spare. Gane's commentary has the same goal but is more satisfying. LM★★★

Bellinger, W. H., Jr. *Leviticus, Numbers*. UBCS. Baker Books, 2001. 338 pp.

This is a fine commentary that provides an interesting and significant reading of the books of Leviticus and Numbers. The series does not allow Bellinger to display it very often, but serious research lies behind his accessible prose. Bellinger does not ignore New Testament connections, but this part could have been strengthened. LM★★↙

Gane, R. *Leviticus, Numbers*. NIVAC. Zondervan/Hodder & Stoughton, 2004. 846 pp.

Gane is an expert in ancient Israelite ritual, and he puts his background to good work in this commentary. He is also adept at pointing to the continuing theological relevance of this material. LM★★★★

Gerstenberger, E. S. *Leviticus*. OTL. Westminster John Knox/ SCM, 1996. 456 pp.

The author situates the material late, to the fifth century BC. He writes very clearly on a level that even laypeople will be able to understand, though some of the technical discussions will not be of interest to them. This is a good, solid commentary from a critical perspective, but other commentaries on the book are better. MS★★★

Harrison, R. K. *Leviticus*. TOTC. InterVarsity, 1980. 252 pp.

Harrison was one of the most competent Old Testament evangelical scholars of the twentieth century. The commentary is too short to compete with Wenham's volume but still well worth having. LM★★★

Hartley, J. E. *Leviticus*. WBC. Nelson/Paternoster, 1992. lxxiii/496 pp.

This commentary is substantial in quality as well as quantity. Hartley approaches his task with the tools of the philologist, literary scholar, and theologian. The approach to authorship is extremely helpful. There is also a lengthy introductory essay on the history of interpretation of the book. MS★★★★★

Hess, R. S. *Leviticus*. REBC 1. Zondervan, 2008. Pp. 563–825.

This commentary is one of the best, most succinct treatments of Leviticus available and is alone worth the price of the volume. Hess is very familiar with Israelite ritual in its ancient Near Eastern context. LM★★★★★

Kiuchi, N. *Leviticus*. AOTC. InterVarsity, 2007. 538 pp.

Kiuchi is an expert on Levitical ritual law as well as a sensitive exegete and theologian. He also considers New Testament perspectives on the material. Highly recommended. MS★★★★★

Knight, G. A. F. *Leviticus*. DSB. Westminster John Knox, 1981. 173 pp.

While moderately critical in his approach to Leviticus, Knight provides a helpful exposition of what the book means in its Old Testament context and devotes considerable attention to its relevance for the Christian. One of the better volumes of the series. LM★★★

Levine, B. A. *Leviticus*. JPS Torah Commentary. Jewish Publication Society, 1989. xlvi/284 pp.

Levine writes with the educated layperson in mind. His writing style is accessible, and he treats topics of interest to the scholar. Levine is one of the true experts on Leviticus and presents a stimulating and important study of the book within its context in the ancient world. He is also theologically sensitive. MS★★★★

Milgrom, J. *Leviticus 1–16*. AYBC. Yale University Press, 1991. *Leviticus 17–22*. AYBC. Yale University Press, 2000. *Leviticus*

23–27. AYBC. Yale University Press, 2001. xviii/1163 pp., xvii/624 pp., and xxi/818 pp.

Milgrom divides Leviticus into three parts. The first volume of his commentary covers the section owing its origin to P; the second volume covers the section that he argues comes from H (the Holiness Code). However, he is most concerned with the final form of the text, not its prehistory. Milgrom is clearly the world's leading expert on Leviticus. He writes from a moderately critical point of view, informed by his wealth of knowledge of early Jewish interpretation. MS★★★★★

Noordtzij, A. *Leviticus*. BSC. Zondervan, 1982. xi/280 pp.

This commentary is a translation of a Dutch original and presents a basic evangelical approach to the text, although Noordtzij believes that some of the laws are post-Mosaic. He is theologically sensitive and responsible. MS★★✦

Radner, E. *Leviticus*. BTCB. Brazos, 2008. 320 pp.

Radner's work is helpful from the vantage point of historical theology—his specialty—and the book of Leviticus. However, if you want a commentary that grapples with the meaning of the book of Leviticus in its ancient setting as a preface to christological and Trinitarian and ecclesial readings, you will have to go elsewhere. MS★★

Rooker, M. F. *Leviticus*. NAC. Broadman, 2000. 352 pp.

Rooker writes in an engaging style and has an eye on making the book relevant for the Christian reader by pointing out connections to New Testament theology. LM★★★★

Snaith, N. H. *Leviticus and Numbers*. NCB. Reprint, Sheffield, 1977. xii/352 pp.

Snaith is a competent Hebraist, so it is not surprising that the strength of this volume is in textual criticism and philology. The commentary suffers from the restraints of the series. It is really a brief, sketchy commentary on the RSV. Although there is little theological reflection, the text is clearly written from a critical perspective. S★★

Wenham, G. J. *The Book of Leviticus.* NICOT. Eerdmans, 1979. xiii/362 pp.

Wenham has provided a fascinating and extremely helpful discussion of what most Christians regard as a drab book. He does an excellent job explaining the holiness laws and their function in ancient Israel. It is a well-written commentary. MS★★★★★

NUMBERS

Ashley, T. R. *The Book of Numbers.* NICOT. Eerdmans, 1993. xvi/667 pp.

While Wenham's short commentary is excellent, the NICOT format allows Ashley to delve more deeply and widely into the issues surrounding this important, though neglected, book of the Pentateuch. Ashley writes in a very readable style. He not only deals with the technical problems of the book but also demonstrates the relevance of the book for theology. He interacts with previous scholarship, but not obsessively. MS★★★★

Bellinger, W. H., Jr. *Leviticus, Numbers.* UBCS. Baker Books, 2001. 338 pp.

See under Leviticus.

Brown, R. *The Message of Numbers.* BST. InterVarsity, 2002. 288 pp.

A readable and informed study of this often-neglected book. In keeping with the series, Brown emphasizes the theological meaning and the contemporary significance of the book. LM★★★

Budd, P. J. *Numbers*. WBC. Nelson/Paternoster, 1984. xxxii/409 pp.

This is a well-researched and thought-out commentary. It employs a source-critical methodology in a way that will offend some evangelicals. It is weak in biblical theology. S★★

Cole, R. D. *Numbers*. NAC. Broadman, 2001. 590 pp.

A substantial, well-written commentary that navigates the scholarly literature well, incorporating what is good and rejecting what is bad, while still keeping its individual contribution. Cole gives an excellent argument in favor of an essential or core Mosaic authorship of Numbers. The book's real strength is in its sensitive theological reading. LM★★★★★

Gane, R. *Leviticus, Numbers*. NIVAC. Zondervan/Hodder & Stoughton, 2004. 846 pp.

See under Leviticus.

Harrison, R. K. *Numbers*. WEC. Moody, 1990. xvi/452 pp.

This commentary takes a verse-by-verse approach (as opposed to Silva's Philippians commentary in the same series). It emphasizes exegesis and exposition with a strong focus on history and Near Eastern background, although there are many insightful theological comments as well. Harrison competently defends a traditionally orthodox approach to the book. However, he often addresses side issues rather than the real heart of the passage at hand. MS★★★

Levine, B. A. *Numbers 1–20*. AYBC. Yale University Press, 1993. *Numbers 21–36*. AYBC. Yale University Press, 2000. xvi/528 pp. and xxii/624 pp.

About Levine's erudition there is no doubt, and all serious students of Numbers must have this book. Levine is not only convinced but also serious about his study of sources in the book of Numbers.

Those more concerned about the final form of the book will find the introductory material especially tedious. S★★★★

Milgrom, J. *Numbers*. JPS Torah Commentary. Jewish Publication Society, 1990. lxi/520 pp.

This commentary is a masterpiece of erudition. The seventy-seven excurses are themselves worth the money. Milgrom gives the reader a careful study of the details and general message of the book. He is concerned to share the insights of medieval Jewish commentators, insights inaccessible to those who do not read postbiblical Hebrew. MS★★★★★

Noordtzij, A. *Numbers*. BSC. Zondervan, 1983. ix/304 pp.

Originally published in Dutch in 1953, this commentary is particularly helpful in the area of theology. Other commentaries would be more helpful in the legal portions of Numbers. MS★↙

Olson, D. T. *Numbers*. Interp. Westminster John Knox, 1996. 196 pp.

No one has had a larger influence in recent years on our understanding of the theological theme of the book of Numbers than Olson. He exposits the book in the light of the theme of wilderness wandering and in the light of the structure formed by the two census accounts in chapters 1 and 26. Here we see judgment on the old generation of rebellion and the rise of the second generation of hope. He does reflect a traditionally critical view that the book essentially was composed after the exile and reflects the concerns of that time. LM★★★★★

Riggans, W. *Numbers*. DSB. Westminster John Knox, 1983. 252 pp.

Riggans does a good job relating the ancient biblical world to the modern one that laypeople readily understand. He emphasizes the theological and practical aspects of Numbers. In keeping with the purpose of the series, he does not get much into introductory issues. LM★★★

Snaith, N. H. *Leviticus and Numbers*. NCB. Reprint, Sheffield, 1977. xii/352 pp.

See under Leviticus.

Stubbs, D. L. *Numbers*. BTCB. Brazos, 2009. 269 pp.

I very much like Stubbs's christological approach to the text, but he doesn't have to ignore the historical dimension of the text to do it. This commentary provides a good second read after a more historically oriented commentary. Even so, there is much of value and interest in this commentary, because he does ground his theological interpretation in the text (not always the case in this series). MS★★★✦

Wenham, G. J. *Numbers*. TOTC. InterVarsity, 1981. 240 pp.

Wenham does a wonderful job making this often-neglected book come alive theologically. It is lamentable that the confines of the series have restricted the length of this commentary. Highly recommended for students, pastors, and scholars. MS★★★★

DEUTERONOMY

Biddle, M. E. *Deuteronomy*. SHBC. Smyth and Helwys, 2003. 535 pp.

A rather uninspiring reading of Deuteronomy. The introduction creates a straw man by suggesting that conservatives believe that Moses wrote every word of the Pentateuch and then opts for the pious fraud theory of Deuteronomy's composition. LM★★

Brown, R. *The Message of Deuteronomy: Not by Bread Alone*. BST. InterVarsity, 1993. 331 pp.

This commentary, written by an English Baptist minister, is very helpful in its attempts to bridge the ancient text and modern social and ethical situations. It is not a deeply researched volume. It also adopts a rather topical theological approach to the text, which has its place, but it could have been much improved by a thematic, biblical-theological analysis. LM★★

Christensen, D. L. *Deuteronomy 1:1–21:9*. WBC. Nelson/Paternoster, 2001. *Deuteronomy 21:10–34:12*. WBC. Nelson/Paternoster, 2002. cxii/458 pp. and li/440 pp.

Christensen first published a commentary on Deuteronomy 1–11 in this series, and the first volume, which covers 1:1–21:9, is a revision and expansion of that earlier work. This commentary is not for the timid. It is technical and also presents new theories about the nature of Deuteronomy. It is too early to call it idiosyncratic, but before the minister or student invests in this commentary over others that may be more helpful in terms of theological message, it is best to let scholars take a few years to sift through his ideas. The low rating reflects this fact and is clearly not a reflection on the author's obvious brilliance. MS★★

Clifford, R. *Deuteronomy with Excursus on Covenant and Law*. OTM. Michael Glazier, 1982. 193 pp.

Clifford, well known for his scholarly articles, dates the book of Deuteronomy late and gives a two-hundred-year period of composition. He identifies the genre of the book as "speech modelled on covenant formulary" (3). The excursus is short but covers an important topic. Readable. LM★★★

Craigie, P. C. *The Book of Deuteronomy*. NICOT. Eerdmans, 1976. 424 pp.

Craigie is among the best of recent evangelical interpreters. His work on Deuteronomy is no exception to the high quality of his work. He is an astute theologian and philologist. He adopts a firmly evangelical approach to the book of Deuteronomy, evident in his insistence on the essential unity of the book based on the treaty analogy. LM★★★

Mayes, A. D. H. *Deuteronomy*. NCB. Sheffield, 1979. 416 pp.

This volume shares some of the shortcomings of the series in that it comments on the RSV and is too brief. It is among the best, however, in the series. Comes from a critical perspective. LM★★★

McConville, J. G. *Deuteronomy*. AOTC. InterVarsity, 2002. 545 pp.

This commentary is in dialogue with modern history of interpretation. Written in an accessible style, it is theologically sensitive and provides a fresh approach that needs serious consideration, though conservatives and critics alike will find obstacles to accepting it. MS★★★⁴

Merrill, E. H. *Deuteronomy*. NAC. Broadman, 1994. 477 pp.

This early contribution in the New American Commentary series is well written and informative. It is particularly noteworthy in its consistent evangelical approach and in its thoroughgoing use of the covenant concept in the exposition of Deuteronomy. The scholarship on which it is based strikes one as a little dated. For instance, the use of the Hittite treaty form for early dating of the book (a conclusion with which I agree) does not take into account the flexible structure of the Hittite treaty itself. MS★★⁴

Miller, P. D., Jr. *Deuteronomy*. Interp. Westminster John Knox, 1990. xv/253 pp.

Miller is theologically concerned and sensitive to literary form in this helpful and well-written study. His approach is moderately critical, and his writing style is engaging. He deals with academic questions and cites previous studies, but his primary concern is with the meaning of the canonical text. M★★★★

Payne, D. F. *Deuteronomy*. DSB. Westminster John Knox, 1985. 197 pp.

Payne writes clearly and nontechnically in this highly informative commentary. He divides the book into more than eighty sections and gives each a catchy title. This commentary remains open to the question of date. Nonetheless, it acknowledges that the book's message is especially relevant to times of political disaster. Payne examines Deuteronomy as a book of law, as a sermon, and as history. LM★★★

Ridderbos, J. *Deuteronomy*. BSC. Zondervan, 1984. 336 pp.

Ridderbos, one of the best Dutch Old Testament scholars of the previous generation, has contributed a formidable conservative defense against critical theories of Deuteronomy. He defends essential Mosaic authorship, while also recognizing the work of a later redactor. In the commentary proper, Ridderbos is theologically sensitive and exegetically insightful. He relates this Old Testament book to our New Testament situation. However, the commentary is now dated and superseded by others that share the same perspective (McConville, Merrill, Wright). LM★★↙

Thompson, J. A. *Deuteronomy*. TOTC. InterVarsity, 1974. 320 pp.

Although brief, this commentary is stimulating and full of helpful information. Thompson makes good use of the treaty analogy to Deuteronomy. He deals with many of the critical issues of the book from an evangelical perspective, includes a thoughtful essay on the difficult question of the book's date, and provides some good discussion of the theology of the book. LM★★★

Tigay, J. H. *Deuteronomy*. JPS Torah Commentary. Jewish Publication Society, 1996. xlix/548 pp.

A well-written and beautifully produced commentary that provides the Hebrew text, a translation, notes, and expository comments. The history of interpretation, particularly in Jewish tradition, is called on to help elucidate the text. The approach to questions of history of composition is a moderately critical one. MS★★★★

von Rad, G. *Deuteronomy*. OTL. Westminster John Knox/SCM, 1966. 211 pp.

Von Rad was one of the chief figures in Old Testament studies in the 1950s and beyond. He helped shape the method of study for the field during that time. This brief (especially considering the central importance of Deuteronomy to von Rad's research) commentary illustrates his approach and many of his most significant conclusions. His approach combines source, form, and redaction criticism. He concludes that while the final form of Deuteronomy is associated with Josiah's reform, the book was the product of northern Levites. S★★★

Weinfeld, M. *Deuteronomy 1–11*. AYBC. Yale University Press, 1991. xiv/448 pp.

The first volume of Weinfeld's commentary illustrates his erudition and insight into this biblical book. Deuteronomy's first eleven chapters, Weinfeld writes, contain history and sermon; the rest of Deuteronomy concentrates on law and will be the focus of the second volume. All the introductory material is found in the first volume (with the exception of the discussion of the text). Weinfeld writes from a critical point of view, believing that much of the material in Deuteronomy is ancient but that it received a major redaction during the Hezekiah and Josiah reforms. There is much interesting literary and theological discussion surrounding the relationship between the book and covenant/loyalty oaths. MS★★★★

Woods, E. J. *Deuteronomy*. TOTC. InterVarsity, 2011. 333 pp.

Woods dates the majority of the book to the time of Moses, which he places in the fifteenth century BC (though he allows for minimal editing after that time). He does so in the light of a thorough knowledge of the issues involved and the extensive scholarly discussion. Though short, the exposition is helpful and clear. LM★★★★

Work, T. *Deuteronomy.* BTCB. Brazos, 2009. 333 pp.

I confess that I worry when theologians write a commentary on a biblical book and I am critical of some of the volumes in this series, but Work remains grounded in the text and does not try to avoid difficult exegetical issues. The result is an often-insightful, fresh look at the book. LM★★★★

Wright, C. K. *Deuteronomy.* UBCS. Baker Books, 1996. 350 pp.

Wright, a well-known biblical ethicist, does well with the book of Deuteronomy with a special emphasis on his area of expertise and interest. He has a refreshing belief in a "substantial Mosaic legacy" of the book. He is sensitive to the book's trajectory to the New Testament. LM★★★★

JOSHUA

Auld, A. G. *Joshua, Judges, and Ruth.* DSB. Westminster John Knox, 1984. 290 pp.

A short but insightful and extremely readable exposition. In a brief introduction, Auld expresses a skeptical view concerning historicity, but his theological sensitivities redeem the volume. LM★★★

Boling, R. G., and G. E. Wright. *Joshua.* AYBC. Yale University Press, 1982. xvii/580 pp.

Wright's untimely death prevented his full participation in this project; most of the work is that of his well-known student Boling (who also did the Judges commentary for this series). The commentary is critical in its approach to the text and theology of Joshua. The history and archaeology of Israel are emphasized. MS★★

Butler, T. *Joshua.* WBC. Nelson/Paternoster, 1983. xliii/304 pp.

This is a well-researched and thought-out commentary, full of philological, textual, and exegetical information and insight. It represents an evangelical, but not traditional, viewpoint on the book. MS★★★★

Creach, J. F. D. *Joshua*. Interp. Westminster John Knox, 2003. 168 pp.

Creach creates an unfortunate divide between Joshua as theology and as history that seriously damages the value of the commentary. Even so, Creach has a lively writing style and provides some helpful literary and theological insights. LM★✔

Dallaire, H. *Joshua*. REBC 2. Zondervan, forthcoming.

Dallaire's commentary will be very helpful to new readers of the book of Joshua. She does a good job delineating the basic message of the book. LM★★★

Goslinga, C. J. *Joshua, Judges, Ruth*. BSC. Zondervan, 1986. 558 pp.

This commentary was translated from a Dutch original that dates from the late 1920s and early 1930s. Although it may not take into account the most recent scholarship, it is an excellent commentary from an evangelical-Reformed standpoint. Strong on theology. MS★★★

Gray, J. *Joshua, Judges, and Ruth*. NCB. Sheffield, 1967; rev. ed., Sheffield/Marshall Pickering, 1986. 427 pp.

Gray follows Noth in attributing both Joshua and Judges to the Deuteronomist (and assumes a seventh-century date for Deuteronomy). He believes that Joshua is of limited value as a historical work, and that Judges is a more sober account of history. S★

Hamlin, E. J. *Joshua: Inheriting the Land*. ITC. Handsel, 1983. xxiii/207 pp.

This is an engagingly written exposition of Joshua that looks at the book as a continuation of the exodus pattern. Hamlin examines the conquest in light of the theme of the liberation of the oppressed and asks how the text is relevant for today. The book imbibes of a moderate historical criticism to make its point. M★★★

Harris, J. G., C. Brown, and M. Moore. *Joshua, Judges, Ruth.* **UBCS. Baker Books, 2000. xxxiii/398 pp.**

Though the authors of the three parts of the book are different, they are aligned in their "canonical historical approach" to their subject matter, with good results. LM★★★

Hess, R. S. *Joshua.* **TOTC. InterVarsity, 1996. 320 pp.**

This is one of the best TOTC commentaries and one of the best commentaries on the book of Joshua. Hess, an acknowledged expert on ancient Near Eastern literature and Israelite history, defends the essential authenticity of the historical memory of the book. He also is an adept interpreter of the literary and theological aspects of the book. LM★★★★★

Hoppe, L. *Joshua, Judges.* **OTM. Michael Glazier, 1982. 218 pp.**

A popularly oriented theological study of the final form of the text. Hoppe helpfully orients his readers to the concept of the Deuteronomic history. He is less successful in dealing with the important theological concept of holy war. LM★★

Howard, D. M., Jr. *Joshua.* **NAC. Broadman, 1998. 464 pp.**

This commentary is one of the best on Joshua, though the field is not particularly strong. Nonetheless, Howard's contribution is well written, well researched, and well thought-out. He adopts a relatively conservative approach to the history that is particularly admirable in this age of skepticism. He is also quite good at pointing out theological themes. LM★★★★

Hubbard, R. L., Jr. *Joshua*. NIVAC. Zondervan, 2009. 652 pp.

Joshua has become the battleground of controversy in the past decade raising theological/ethical questions with its picture of God as a warrior and historical issues in connection with archaeology as to whether its picture of Israel's entry into the land is accurately depicted in the book. Hubbard, a seasoned commentator (see Ruth), has well navigated these difficult waters. His commentary opens up the theological teaching and contemporary significance of Joshua. LM★★★★★

McConville, J. G., and S. N. Williams. *Joshua*. THOTC. Eerdmans, 2010. xii/257 pp.

An eminently worthwhile volume to read even though many of its theological reflections and historical musings are problematic (at least to this reviewer). The book waffles on the question of historicity and, to use one example, pits the Jesus of the Gospels against the God depicted in Joshua and the Jesus of Revelation in matters of holy war. Again, if you want a stimulating read (much of which I hope you disagree with), this book is for you. MS★★★

Miller, J. M., and G. M. Tucker. *The Book of Joshua*. CBC. Cambridge University Press, 1974. x/206 pp.

The authors give a careful description of the literary composition of the book from a critical perspective. They concentrate on the Deuteronomistic redaction, which they think is the strongest voice in the book. They exaggerate supposed contradictions in the book and use archaeology to inform their commentary. LM★★

Nelson, R. *Joshua*. OTL. Westminster John Knox/SCM, 1997. xviii/310 pp.

Nelson has a low view of the historical worth of the book. He employs both diachronic as well as synchronic analyses, but the commentary has a kind of "old school" critical feel. S★★

Soggin, J. A. *Joshua*. OTL. Westminster John Knox/SCM, 1972. xvii/245 pp.

Soggin, an Italian scholar writing in the German tradition, emphasizes historical and archaeological studies. There is not much theological comment. S★★

Woudstra, M. *The Book of Joshua*. NICOT. Eerdmans, 1981. xiv/396 pp.

Woudstra gives a very good exegetical analysis of the book. He also has an excellent biblical-theological sense. There are some good literary observations, but much more could be done in this area. LM★★ↄ

JUDGES

Auld, A. G. *Joshua, Judges, and Ruth*. DSB. Westminster John Knox, 1984. 290 pp.

See under Joshua.

Block, D. I. *Judges, Ruth*. NAC. Broadman, 1999. 765 pp.

This substantial contribution is clearly the best thing available on the book of Judges. Block is thoroughly aware of all the literature that precedes him, and he incorporates what is good and criticizes what is bad. His own perspective may be idiosyncratic on rare occasions, but it is usually very insightful. This commentary is particularly strong in literary and theological analysis. LM★★★★★

Boda, M. J. *Judges*. REBC 2. Zondervan, forthcoming.

This insightful commentary is extremely helpful in unpacking the message of the book of Judges. Boda is an excellent scholar of the history, literature, and theology of the Old Testament and puts his expertise to good work unpacking this interesting and sometimes enigmatic book. LM★★★★★

Boling, R. G. *Judges*. AYBC. Yale University Press, 1975. xxi/338 pp.

This volume is perhaps one of the most well-known recent commentaries on the book of Judges. It is competently written from a critical perspective with an emphasis on history, comparative studies, and philology. Boling suggests a peasant-revolt model of the conquest and believes that Israel's early social structure is similar to Greek amphictyonies. He also utilizes the covenant-treaty analogy. There is not much in the way of literary or theological reflection, as is typical of the series. MS★★★

Butler, T. *Judges*. WBC. Nelson, 2009. xcii/538 pp.

Butler gives thorough discussion of all the important issues and interacts with the leading scholarship on the book. His own views are mostly persuasive. He reaches largely a positive conclusion about Judges as a historical testimony to the period and has an excellent sensitivity to the theological significance of the book. MS★★★★★

Cundall, A. E., and L. Morris. *Judges and Ruth*. TOTC. InterVarsity, 1968. 318 pp.

Cundall's section on Judges is an adequate, but not outstanding, treatment of that book. He argues for a conservative position on the historicity of Judges and Joshua, believing the two books give complementary, and not contradictory, perspectives on the conquest. LM★★

Goslinga, C. J. *Joshua, Judges, Ruth*. BSC. Zondervan, 1986. 558 pp.

See under Joshua.

Gray, J. *Joshua, Judges, and Ruth*. NCB. Sheffield, 1967; rev. ed., Sheffield/Marshall Pickering, 1986. 427 pp.

See under Joshua.

Harris, J. G., C. Brown, and M. Moore. *Joshua, Judges, Ruth.* UBCS. Baker Books, 2000. xxxiii/398 pp.

See under Joshua.

Niditch, S. *Judges.* OTL. Westminster John Knox, 2008. xxviii/290 pp.

Niditch is well known for her study of oral literature and folklore, and she applies her knowledge of such to the book of Judges. While there is much of interest for the scholar even when one might disagree with her analysis, this commentary is not recommended for ministers and laypeople. S★★★

Soggin, J. A. *Judges.* OTL. Westminster John Knox/SCM, 1981. xx/305 pp.

Once again, as in his commentary on Joshua, Soggin concentrates on critical and historical issues. He consciously avoids making theological statements. However, this is a more mature and profitable commentary than his earlier commentary on Joshua. S★★★

Wilcock, M. *The Message of Judges: Grace Abounding.* BST. Inter-Varsity, 1992. 175 pp.

Wilcock provides an interesting retelling of the story of Judges. He makes the story come alive for the lay reader and also derives moral and behavioral principles from the book. This is not the commentary for technical information about the book, and it is not particularly satisfying for theological meditation. LM★★★

Younger, K. L., Jr. *Judges/Ruth.* NIVAC. Zondervan/Hodder & Stoughton, 2002. 511 pp.

See under Ruth.

RUTH

Atkinson, D. *The Message of Ruth: The Wings of Refuge*. BST. InterVarsity, 1983. 128 pp.

Atkinson is as interesting a writer here as he is in his Genesis 1–11 commentary. He gives some stimulating illustrations as he exposits the major themes of the book. He focuses on providence. LM★★★

Auld, A. G. *Joshua, Judges, and Ruth*. DSB. Westminster John Knox, 1984. 290 pp.

See under Joshua.

Block, D. I. *Judges, Ruth*. NAC. Broadman, 1999. 765 pp.

See under Judges.

Bush, F. W. *Ruth/Esther*. WBC. Nelson/Paternoster, 1996. xiv/514 pp.

See under Esther.

Campbell, E. F., Jr. *Ruth*. AYBC. Yale University Press, 1975. xx/189 pp.

This is a very stimulating and well-written commentary. Campbell explores many of the ancient social conventions that lie behind the text (levirate marriage, the kinsman redeemer, the removal of the sandal). He provides an early example of literary analysis. MS★★★

Cundall, A. E., and L. Morris. *Judges and Ruth*. TOTC. InterVarsity, 1968. 318 pp.

See under Judges. Morris, a New Testament scholar, comments on Ruth. He shows a good knowledge of the Old Testament and its background. LM★★

Goslinga, C. J. *Joshua, Judges, Ruth.* BSC. Zondervan, 1986. 558 pp.

See under Joshua.

Gray, J. *Joshua, Judges, and Ruth.* NCB. Sheffield, 1967; rev. ed., Sheffield/Marshall Pickering, 1986. 427 pp.

See under Joshua.

Harris, J. G., C. Brown, and M. Moore. *Joshua, Judges, Ruth.* UBCS. Baker Books, 2000. xxxiii/398 pp.

See under Joshua.

Hubbard, R. L., Jr. *The Book of Ruth.* NICOT. Eerdmans, 1988. xiv/317 pp.

This commentary's introduction is extensive and profitable as it discusses issues of unity, theology, canonicity, text, and more. The commentary as a whole demonstrates careful scholarship, a lively writing style, and balanced judgment. Hubbard pays attention to all aspects of the book of Ruth. This commentary is one of the very best of the series. MS★★★★★

Murphy, R. E. *Wisdom Literature: Job, Proverbs, Ruth, Canticles, Ecclesiastes, and Esther.* FOTL. Eerdmans, 1981. 185 pp.

See under Job.

Nielsen, K. *Ruth.* OTL. Westminster John Knox/SCM, 1997. xiv/106 pp.

Generically, Nielsen believes that Ruth, with its connection between narrative and genealogy, is most like the patriarchal narratives. She employs intertextuality and analyzes Ruth's use of earlier biblical tradition. In particular, she finds the story of Tamar in Genesis 38 especially illuminating. She presents an interesting description of her hermeneutical theory in the introduction. The intention of Ruth is to counter a smear campaign against David that shows he is descended from a Moabite, but the book shows that this is all the will of Yahweh. MS★★★

Sakenfeld, K. D. *Ruth*. Interp. Westminster John Knox, 1999. xii/91 pp.

Though a relatively short commentary—even for a short book like Ruth—Sakenfeld has provided a great deal of insight into both the theological and sociological significance of the book. LM★★★★

Sasson, J. M. *Ruth: A New Translation with a Philological Commentary and a Formalist-Folklorist Interpretation*. 2nd ed. Sheffield Academic Press, 1989. xviii/292 pp.

This major scholarly study needs to be consulted on philological matters. Sasson shows great literary sensitivity, depending on V. Propp for formal analysis. The commentary is a repository of discussion on the book. S★★★★

Younger, K. L., Jr. *Judges/Ruth*. NIVAC. Zondervan/Hodder & Stoughton, 2002. 511 pp.

Younger is an insightful and learned student of the Old Testament, and he does a good job in particular with the "original meaning" section of the commentary. He describes well Ruth's historical background, literary devices, and theological message. He is often insightful but not as strong on the "contemporary significance" of the book. LM★★★↙

SAMUEL

Anderson, A. A. *2 Samuel*. WBC. Nelson/Paternoster, 1989. xl/302 pp.

This commentary is thoroughly researched and meticulously presented. Anderson does a good job presenting the critical issues of the book and also expressing his own moderately critical perspective. He does an especially good job dealing with the important text-critical problem of the book. The bibliographies are well done. A number of unfortunate typographical errors can be found. MS★★✦

Arnold, B. T. *1 and 2 Samuel*. NIVAC. Zondervan/Hodder & Stoughton, 2003. 681 pp.

Arnold, a seasoned interpreter of the Old Testament, does an excellent job revealing the original meaning of this text and bringing it to life for the modern reader. LM★★★✦

Auld, A. G. *I and II Samuel*. OTL. Westminster John Knox, 2011. xxii/686 pp.

Auld recognizes that the book of Samuel is "all about David" (2). One of the main concerns of the commentary is on the interesting (to the scholar and few others) question of the textual traditions of the book, and his intentionally literal translation of both the Greek and Masoretic traditions allows the reader to distinguish the two. Exposition of the book is strong, but there is little broader theological reflection. S★★★✦

Baldwin, J. G. *1 and 2 Samuel*. TOTC. InterVarsity, 1988. 299 pp.

Baldwin's commentary is characterized by careful scholarship. She writes with the educated lay reader in mind. In the introduction, she critiques some critical theories of composition (Wellhausen and Noth). She leaves the question up in the air, since the biblical material is not specific. The emphasis of the commentary is on exegesis and theology. LM★★✦

Bergen, R. D. *1, 2 Samuel*. NAC. Broadman, 1996. 416 pp.

Bergen's is a competent and readable treatment of the narrative of Samuel, sensitive to historical, literary, and theological issues. LM★★★

Brueggemann, W. *First and Second Samuel*. Interp. Westminster
John Knox, 1990. x/362 pp.

Brueggemann, who produced the highly regarded Genesis commentary in this series, has produced a fascinating study of Samuel.
His writing style is not just engaging but also exciting. He is a moderate critic who takes a canonical approach to the text. LM★★★★

Campbell, A. F. *1 Samuel*. FOTL. Eerdmans, 2003. xviii/350 pp.

An intelligent and interesting contribution to the series. It is increas-
ingly my contention that the series, and this volume, are, despite
the introduction, of importance to the scholarly community but
not the lay or ministerial communities. S★★✦

Conroy, C. *1–2 Samuel; 1–2 Kings, with an Excursus on Davidic
Dynasty and Holy City Zion*. OTM. Michael Glazier, 1983.
266 pp.

Conroy has written competently on a scholarly level on Samuel
before doing this commentary. He is sensitive to the book as literature. He has an excursus on David and Zion in the Old Testament,
but could have developed the New Testament connections more
extensively. LM★★★

Evans, M. J. *1 and 2 Samuel*. UBCS. Baker Books, 2000.
xiv/267 pp.

Her analysis of Samuel focuses on the role of power, its "nature,
accession, use, and abuse" (9). She has a good literary sense, particularly in her analysis of the plot and characterization of the
narrative. LM★★★

Firth, D. G. *1 and 2 Samuel*. AOTC. InterVarsity, 2009. 614 pp.

Firth is sensitive to literary concerns, serious about the book's
historical issues, and insightful on its theological teaching. He
sees the major themes of the book as divine and human kingship

as well as prophetic authority. All in all a very worthwhile commentary. MS★★★★★

Gordon, R. P. *1 and 2 Samuel*. Library of Biblical Interpretation. Zondervan, 1988. 375 pp.

This commentary is a refreshing literary reading of Samuel. It is full of good theological insight and occasional philological and textual comments. MS★★★★

Hertzberg, H. W. *I and II Samuel*. OTL. Westminster John Knox/SCM, 1964. 416 pp.

A good exegetical commentary from a critical perspective. Not much theological help. MS★★

Jobling, D. *1 Samuel*. Berit Olam. Michael Glazier, 1998. x/330 pp.

This commentary is written from a postmodern, eclectic standpoint. The best use of this book is to read it to see how such a hermeneutic influences one's reading rather than to use it for exploring the meaning of Samuel. MS★⸽

Klein, R. W. *I Samuel*. WBC. Nelson/Paternoster, 1983. xxxiii/307 pp.

This commentary is particularly helpful as a guide to the text-critical, philological, and historical issues of 1 Samuel. Textual issues are particularly important for this book. Klein has chosen not to concentrate on literary or theological issues, and this choice weakens the commentary. MS★★★

Mauchline, J. *1 and 2 Samuel*. NCB. Sheffield, 1971. 336 pp.

Mauchline's commentary suffers from the limits of this series. It is a commentary on the RSV and too short. Of very little help. S★

McCarter, P. K., Jr. *I Samuel*. AYBC. Yale University Press, 1980. *II Samuel*. AYBC. Yale University Press, 1984. xii/475 pp. and xviii/553 pp.

McCarter is the most competent text critic to deal with Samuel, although in his conclusions Klein is probably better since he tends to stick with the MT more often (and this appears warranted by the evidence). McCarter, however, had access to the Dead Sea Scrolls of Samuel. Although written from a critical perspective, this commentary is well worth having. MS★★⌿

Murphy, F. A. *1 Samuel*. BTCB. Brazos, 2010. 299 pp.

All I can say is that I don't know what Murphy is talking about, but it's not the text of 1 Samuel. I can't recommend this commentary for anyone. No stars.

Payne, D. F. *I and II Samuel*. DSB. Westminster John Knox, 1982. viii/278 pp.

Payne's style is very accessible, in the tradition of DSB. He makes ancient customs understandable and emphasizes a theological exposition. He identifies the leading theme of 1 and 2 Samuel as leadership—a theme that anticipates Christ. LM★★★

Tsumura, D. T. *The First Book of Samuel*. NICOT. Eerdmans, 2007. xxii/698 pp.

Tsumura's strengths are in the areas of history and grammatical study (using discourse analysis for the above-the-sentence level). Interestingly, he sticks with the Masoretic textual tradition in a book where there seems to be growing awareness that this text has suffered from some textual transmission problems that can be remedied by appeal to the Qumran and Septuagint material. The publication of his manuscript might have been delayed; the bibliography shows that the most recent secondary literature comes from before 2001. S★★★

Youngblood, R. F. *1 and 2 Samuel*. REBC 3. Zondervan, 2009. Pp. 23–614.

A solid commentary that shows good exegetical sense and literary and theological sensitivity. While it is not substantially updated from the original edition, it nonetheless maintains good value as it insightfully exposits the message of the book. LM★★★✔

KINGS

Auld, A. G. *Kings*. DSB. Westminster John Knox, 1986. 259 pp.

Auld gives a clear, simple exposition of the text. He emphasizes meaning and application. LM★★★

Brueggemann, W. *1 and 2 Kings*. SHBC. Smyth and Helwys, 2000. 645 pp.

Brueggemann is always interesting and insightful and this, the inaugural volume in a new series, does not disappoint. Brueggemann is always asking questions that are relevant to church and society today. It is an easy read and even a commentary series with illustrations! LM★★★★

Cogan, M. *I Kings*. AYBC. Yale University Press, 2001. xvii/556 pp.

Cogan along with H. Tadmor produced the volume on 2 Kings twelve years before. This volume is Cogan's alone and includes the introduction to the whole promised in the earlier volume. Like the previous contribution, this one also emphasizes history and ancient Near Eastern background but is also sensitive to literary qualities. Especially interesting is his discussion of sources of Kings in the introduction. S★★★★

Cogan, M., and H. Tadmor. *II Kings*. AYBC. Yale University Press, 1988. xxxv/371 pp.

Cogan and Tadmor are historically oriented experts in Mesopotamian studies. Thus it is not surprising that they concentrate on the Mesopotamian historical backdrop of the book. S★★★★

DeVries, S. *I Kings*. 2nd ed. WBC. Nelson/Paternoster, 2003 (1st ed., Nelson/Paternoster, 1985). lxxix/286 pp.

DeVries takes a traditionally critical approach to the book of Kings. He is heavy on source, form, and redaction criticism. These critical methods have an important function to play if used correctly. Unfortunately, they are abused here. There is very little theological or exegetical insight. The second edition is identical with the first but adds a supplemental bibliography on pages lxv–lxxix. S★★

Fritz, V. *1 and 2 Kings*. CC. Fortress, 2003. 462 pp.

Fritz looks at Kings as part of the Deuteronomistic History. The volume is strong on archaeology. However, Fritz sees little historical value in Kings. He provides a very short introduction. MS★★★

Gray, J. *I and II Kings*. OTL. Westminster John Knox/SCM, 1963. 744 pp.

This has been the classic commentary on Kings for the past forty years. Gray presents especially detailed work on chronology and sources from a critical perspective. There is not much theological commentary. S★★★

Hobbs, T. R. *2 Kings*. WBC. Nelson/Paternoster, 1985. xlviii/388 pp.

A well-written and insightful commentary. Its helpful methodological presupposition is that 2 Kings is the work of one author. Hobbs utilizes the literary approach to great benefit. MS★★★★

House, P. R. *1, 2 Kings*. NAC. Broadman, 1995. 432 pp.

The introduction to the commentary gives an excellent and clear exposition of the issues surrounding the interpretation of the book. House gives a good résumé of the secondary literature as well as his own ideas. In particular, he argues that a major theological theme of the book is the presentation and protection of monotheism. LM★★★★

Hubbard, R. L., Jr. *First and Second Kings*. EvBC. Moody, 1991. 240 pp.

Hubbard gives us an excellent popular commentary on this most interesting of historical books. He provides a very helpful entry into the theological significance of this recounting of Israel's past. The introduction would have been helped by further exploration of the relationship between Kings and Deuteronomy. LM★★★★

Jones, G. H. *1 and 2 Kings*. 2 vols. NCB. Sheffield, 1985. lii/666 pp.

This two-volume commentary is one of the best in the series. In the first place, the commentary is proportionally longer than most volumes in NCB, allowing for fuller comment. Jones has a more extensive introduction and bibliography, which also increases the commentary's value. LM★★★

Konkel, A. H. *1 and 2 Kings*. NIVAC. Zondervan/Hodder & Stoughton, 2006. 704 pp.

Readable and insightful, Konkel has produced a commentary on Kings that appeals particularly to pastors who want to preach the text showing the continuing relevance of this book for today. LM★★★★

Leithart, P. *1 and 2 Kings*. BTCB. Brazos, 2006. 304 pp.

A fascinating reading of Kings from an ecclesial, christological (evangelical), and theological point of view. Sometimes I wish he appreciated the message from an Old Testament perspective first, but there are many helpful insights for a Christian reading of Kings. MS★★★★

Long, B. O. *I Kings with an Introduction to Historical Literature*. FOTL. Eerdmans, 1984. xv/265 pp.

Long provides a thoughtful study of the book of Kings and the nature of Israelite historiographical literature from a critical theological perspective. It is particularly gratifying that he is attuned to contemporary literary theory. From an evangelical point of view, his view of the historicity of the text is low. S★★★

Nelson, R. *First and Second Kings*. Interp. Westminster John Knox, 1987. 252 pp.

In keeping with the series, Nelson, a respected scholar on Kings, concentrates on theology and literature, not history. Among other things, he emphasizes the connection with the world of Deuteronomy. He writes in a vivid and engaging style. M★★★★

Patterson, R. D., and H. J. Austel. *1 and 2 Kings*. REBC 3. Zondervan, 2009. Pp. 615–954.

A competent and helpful study of Kings. Patterson is especially known for his sensitivity to literary matters. The commentary is brief, even for the series (compare Youngblood's Samuel in the same volume). I would have liked to see more development of theological themes. LM★★★

Provan, I. W. *1 and 2 Kings*. UBCS. Baker Books, 1995. xiv/306 pp.

In its perspective and readability, this is certainly the best available commentary on Kings. The writing is very accessible, and the emphasis is on literary and theological issues, though the notes also address particular exegetical issues. Too bad that, in keeping with the series, the treatment is necessarily brief. LM★★★★★

Walsh, J. T. *1 Kings*. Berit Olam. Michael Glazier, 1996. xxi/393 pp.

Walsh provides a narrative reading of 1 Kings. He brackets issues of history and retells the biblical story with the aid of recent insights into the conventions of biblical storytelling. Sometimes the commentary is more like a paraphrase of the biblical account. At other times, interesting insight into the text is provided. LM★★★

Wiseman, D. J. *1 and 2 Kings*. TOTC. InterVarsity, 1993. 318 pp.

D. J. Wiseman is greatly appreciated for his important work on ancient Near Eastern literature and for his interest in archaeology. These interests are emphasized in his analysis of Kings and are a tremendous strength of the volume. However, Wiseman is not as interested nor as incisive a commentator on the theological and literary aspects of the text. LM★★★

CHRONICLES

Braun, R. *1 Chronicles*. WBC. Nelson/Paternoster, 1986. xlv/311 pp.

A very helpful discussion of all aspects of the book. Good bibliographies, sensitive exegesis, and helpful comments on Old Testament theology. MS★★✔

Curtis, E. L. *Chronicles*. ICC. T&T Clark, 1910. xxii/534 pp.

Curtis has a low view of Chronicles's historical value. He believes it is unhistorical. He does not prize Chronicles's priestly theology. He does provide a scholarly and extensive discussion of the text of Chronicles, but this is dated. S★

DeVries, S. *1 and 2 Chronicles*. FOTL. Eerdmans, 1989. xv/439 pp.

As with the other commentaries in the series, DeVries concentrates on the structure, genre, and intention of the book. This volume is up-to-date and provides a good perspective on contemporary scholarly opinion on Chronicles. The bibliographies are of special value. S★★

Dillard, R. B. *II Chronicles*. WBC. Nelson/Paternoster, 1987. xxiii/323 pp.

This commentary makes 2 Chronicles come alive. It is superb in its analysis of the theological message, given 2 Chronicles's composition in the postexilic period. It is one of the few Old Testament commentaries that explores connections with the New Testament. MS★★★★★

Hill, A. E. *1 and 2 Chronicles*. NIVAC. Zondervan/Hodder & Stoughton, 2003. 699 pp.

Hill advocates understanding the book of Chronicles as a sermon. This view does not undermine his confidence in the book as a work of history, but he believes that Israel's story is here being applied to the situation of the original audience (God's people sometime between 450 and 400 BC). This perspective is particularly helpful in this commentary because the series calls on him to apply the ancient book to a modern context. LM★★★✦

Japhet, S. *I and II Chronicles*. OTL. Westminster John Knox/ SCM, 1993. xxv/1077 pp.

This masterful commentary covers the bases on the book of Chronicles: philology, text, literary strategy, and history. Its weakest point is theology, but this commentary is a must for all serious students. There is extensive discussion of the secondary literature. Japhet is critical in her thinking, but moderately so, and she arrives at a number of relatively conservative conclusions. MS★★★★★

Knoppers, G. *1 Chronicles*. AYBC. Yale University Press, 2002. *2 Chronicles*. AYBC. Yale University Press, 2004. 544 pp. and 560 pp.

Written with great detail and erudition. Knoppers navigates well many of the critical issues of the book (relationship with Ezra/

Nehemiah, text criticism, use of earlier biblical texts). He presents the view that Chronicles is well understood as "rewritten Bible," but does not provide much theological reflection, in keeping with the purpose of the series. S★★★✦

Mabie, F. J. *1 and 2 Chronicles*. REBC 4. Zondervan, 2010. Pp. 23–336.

Mabie writes in a clear, informative style. He is sensitive to literary and theological contours of the book. While he admirably tries to avoid minimizing Chronicles's unique contributions by overdoing synoptic issues, it may have helped him bring out the former by paying a bit more attention to the latter. LM★★★✦

McConville, J. G. *I and II Chronicles*. DSB. Westminster John Knox, 1984. 280 pp.

This commentary is an interesting and solid exposition of an often-neglected book. McConville is sensitive to theology and application. LM★★★★

Myers, J. M. *1 and 2 Chronicles*. 2 vols. AYBC. Yale University Press, 1965. xciv/241 pp. and 267 pp.

Myers concentrates on issues of history and text and is of very little help in the area of theology. Recent commentaries are much better. S★★

Selman, M. J. *1 Chronicles*. TOTC. InterVarsity, 1994. *2 Chronicles*. TOTC. InterVarsity, 1994. 263 pp. and 286 pp.

Though the whole commentary is relatively short for a book (in two parts) of this size, the introduction is lengthy and helpful. Selman presents a strong case for why the book of Chronicles makes an important contribution to the canon. LM★★★★

Thompson, J. A. *1, 2 Chronicles*. NAC. Broadman, 1994. 410 pp.

Thompson's is a competent, easy-to-read study of Chronicles, with an emphasis on the theological meaning of the book. However, compared to Braun, Dillard, Williamson, and others, there is not much new or exciting here. LM★★★

Tuell, S. S. *First and Second Chronicles*. Interp. Westminster John Knox, 2001. xii/252 pp.

Tuell believes that Chronicles is an "extended meditation on the Hebrew scriptures" (7) with an emphasis on David and the worship in the temple. One of the important messages of Chronicles is to encourage the study of Scripture as that which brings divine blessing. LM★★★

Wilcock, M. *The Message of Chronicles: One Church, One Faith, One Lord*. BST. InterVarsity, 1987. 288 pp.

Wilcock's popular commentary on Chronicles makes much of the fact that the biblical book is sermonic history. Wilcock's writing style is good, and he competently brings out the ancient text's message for today. LM★★★★

Williamson, H. G. M. *1 and 2 Chronicles*. NCB. Sheffield, 1982. xix/428 pp.

In spite of the limitations of the series, this is a very good commentary. Williamson is a well-known expert in postexilic matters and brings his formidable knowledge to bear on the text of Chronicles. MS★★★★

EZRA AND NEHEMIAH

Blenkinsopp, J. *Ezra–Nehemiah*. OTL. Westminster John Knox/SCM, 1988. 366 pp.

Blenkinsopp is one of the leading scholars of the postexilic period, and his erudition comes to the fore in this excellent volume. He informs the reader of contemporary scholarship but does not always agree with the current opinion (see, for instance, his view on the relation of these books to the Chronicler). He also asserts the need for diachronic analysis as well as a more literary or canonical approach. MS★★★

Breneman, M. *Ezra, Nehemiah, Esther*. NAC. Broadman, 1993. 383 pp.

Breneman has produced a competent and readable commentary on these three short and late biblical books. He gives good, simple descriptions of the historical backgrounds of the stories. A popular presentation of some of the most important scholarly decisions on the books. LM★★★

Brockington, L. H. *Ezra, Nehemiah, and Esther*. NCB. Sheffield, 1969. 189 pp.

Brockington's introduction displays a typical critical approach to the books. His comments on the text are sparse, as is usual in this series. MS★★

Clines, D. J. A. *Ezra, Nehemiah, Esther*. NCB. Sheffield, 1984. 342 pp.

In his typical manner, Clines presents a carefully and thoroughly researched commentary. His writing is both scholarly and clear. He carefully presents the important and debated issues of historical background. There is also an excellent study of Esther's historicity. LM★★★★

Fensham, F. C. *The Books of Ezra and Nehemiah*. NICOT. Eerdmans, 1982. xiii/288 pp.

This commentary is traditional in its approach to these two books. For instance, it accepts the view that Ezra arrived in Palestine in 458 BC before Nehemiah, who arrived in 445 BC. Fensham further argues that the Chronicler was responsible for both Ezra and Nehemiah. The emphasis of this volume is on history and culture, but other aspects, like philology and theology, are treated as well. MS★★★

Kidner, D. *Ezra and Nehemiah*. TOTC. InterVarsity, 1979. 174 pp.

This volume is similar in approach to the Fensham commentary but much less scholarly in tone (although the scholarship is there to back it up). It is thus easy to read and emphasizes theology and history. LM★★★

Levering, M. *Ezra and Nehemiah*. BTCB. Brazos, 2007. 236 pp.

Though not a replacement for a good commentary that takes into account the literary and historical dimensions of the text, Levering provides much food for thought in his mainly theological and canonical reading of Ezra/Nehemiah. MS★★★⁄

McConville, J. G. *Ezra, Nehemiah, and Esther*. DSB. Westminster John Knox, 1985. xii/197 pp.

This volume is readable and scholarly without being overly academic. McConville is excellent at both revealing the books' meaning in their Old Testament context and explaining their relevance for today. LM★★★

Myers, J. M. *Ezra, Nehemiah*. AYBC. Yale University Press, 1965. lxxxiii/267 pp.

Myers concentrates on a critical reconstruction of the time period reflected in these two books. The commentary is weak in the areas of philology, literary structure, style, and theology. S★

Throntveit, M. A. *Ezra–Nehemiah*. Interp. Westminster John Knox, 1992. xiii/129 pp.

This easy-to-read yet profound commentary takes full advantage of recent work on these two biblical books without bogging down the reader in too many footnotes. It emphasizes and combines literary analysis and theological message, while downplaying the historical issues of the books. It avoids a typical moralistic reading of the books as well. LM★★★★

Williamson, H. G. M. *Ezra–Nehemiah.* WBC. Nelson/Paternoster, 1985. xix/428 pp.

This is a comprehensive, scholarly commentary written by a highly competent evangelical scholar. Williamson is a lecturer at Cambridge University, and his research specialty is postexilic literature. Although scholarly, this book is helpful to laypeople as well. MS★★★★★

Yamauchi, E. M. *Ezra and Nehemiah.* REBC 4. Zondervan, 2010. Pp. 337–568.

Yamauchi has established himself as one of the world's leading experts on the Persian period, the period of time during which Ezra and Nehemiah lived. One cannot find a better historically oriented commentary than this one, though the literary and theological insights are a bit thin. LM★★★↓

ESTHER

Baldwin, J. G. *Esther.* TOTC. InterVarsity, 1984. 126 pp.

Baldwin combines a keen literary and theological sense with a firm and intelligent opinion concerning the book's historicity. The commentary is well written and based upon thorough research. LM★★★★

Berlin, A. *Esther.* JPS Bible Commentary. Jewish Publication Society, 2001. lix/110 pp.

Berlin is one of the best commentary writers around. Not that she is always correct, but she is an insightful, clear, and interesting writer. She excels at literary analysis, though readers might well dispute her genre identification of the book as a festive comedy, that is, a book that provokes laughter and creates a story set in the Persian period in order to establish Purim. MS★★★★★

Breneman, M. *Ezra, Nehemiah, Esther*. NAC. Broadman, 1993. 383 pp.

See under Ezra and Nehemiah.

Brockington, L. H. *Ezra, Nehemiah, and Esther*. NCB. Sheffield, 1969. 189 pp.

See under Ezra and Nehemiah.

Bush, F. W. *Ruth/Esther*. WBC. Nelson/Paternoster, 1996. xiv/514 pp.

This is one of the most extensive commentaries written on these two short books. It is very competent but tends to be a bit technical. Bush is particularly good at philology. He gives a thorough discussion of all the technical issues. MS★★★★★

Jobes, K. *Esther*. NIVAC. Zondervan/Hodder & Stoughton, 1999. 248 pp.

Without a doubt this is the best commentary to buy on Esther. It is informative about its original meaning and insightful on how to apply it to the contemporary world. Jobes is theologically astute and a good writer. LM★★★★★

Levenson, J. D. *Esther*. OTL. Westminster John Knox/SCM, 1997. xvi/142 pp.

This commentary provides a readable and often-interesting interpretation of Esther that is well versed in the ancient and modern scholarly literature. It also pays attention to the Greek version of the story that is significantly different from the Hebrew version and that is accepted by Catholics as authoritative. Levenson believes that Esther seems well aware of authentic Persian customs and history, but in the final analysis he believes it is a work of historical fiction. MS★★★★

McConville, J. G. *Ezra, Nehemiah, and Esther.* DSB. Westminster John Knox, 1985. xii/197 pp.

See under Ezra and Nehemiah.

Moore, C. A. *Esther.* AYBC. Yale University Press, 1971. xiv/118 pp.

A competent commentary on the book from a non-evangelical perspective. There is a lengthy introductory section with helpful discussions of the problematic issues of canonicity and historicity. The commentary section proper is more balanced than some of the others (for instance, Myers on Chronicles) in the series. MS★★

Murphy, R. E. *Wisdom Literature: Job, Proverbs, Ruth, Canticles, Ecclesiastes, and Esther.* FOTL. Eerdmans, 1981. 185 pp.

See under Job.

Phillips, E. *Esther.* REBC 4. Zondervan, 2010. Pp. 569–674.

A very helpful short commentary on the book, done by a very competent Hebrew Bible scholar. Still, for theological insight, Jobes is to be preferred. LM★★★✦

Reid, D. *Esther.* TOTC. InterVarsity, 2008. 168 pp.

One of the first of the second series of TOTC commentaries to be published. Reid gives a smart, to-the-point interpretation of the book that does not lead astray. Recommended for those who want a brief but helpful exposition of the book. LM★★★★✦

JOB

Alden, R. L. *Job.* NAC. Broadman, 1993. 464 pp.

Alden presents a readable and insightful theological interpretation of the book of Job. He fails, however, to recognize the central issue of the book, which is the nature and origin of wisdom. Nonetheless, much can be learned from this volume. LM★★

Andersen, F. I. *Job.* TOTC. InterVarsity, 1976. 294 pp.

This is one of the best conservative commentaries on Job. It is limited by the length restrictions of the series but still extremely valuable as a lay commentary. LM★★★

Atkinson, D. *The Message of Job: Suffering and Grace.* BST. InterVarsity, 1991. 188 pp.

This commentary provides a very practical approach to Job. Atkinson offers little analysis of the ancient message of the book, but he does show how one major theme connects with our world. LM★✦

Bergant, D. *Job, Ecclesiastes.* OTM. Michael Glazier, 1982. 295 pp.

A good popularly written and moderately critical commentary on the book of Job. In exposition, Bergant "has decided to favor those themes, images and literary forms that cluster around the broad concept of order" (23). LM★✦

Clines, D. J. A. *Job 1–20.* WBC. Nelson/Paternoster, 1989. *Job 21–37.* WBC. Nelson/Paternoster, 2006. *Job 37–42.* WBC. Nelson/Paternoster, 2011. cxi/501 pp., xxiv/532 pp., and xxxv/500 pp.

Clines has written a stimulating and insightful commentary on the book of Job. It is stimulating in the sense that it will get the reader thinking about the book and its issues. It is provocatively written. It is strong in literary and theological analysis. It is long because he extensively discusses linguistic, philological, and textual issues. The bibliographies are incredibly good. MS★★★★✦

Gibson, J. C. L. *Job.* DSB. Westminster John Knox, 1985. ix/284 pp.

Gibson honestly reports that, even after several decades of study, he still struggles with the meaning of the book of Job. Although from a critical perspective, his comments will help readers struggle through this difficult biblical book themselves. LM★★★

Gordis, R. *The Book of Job: Commentary, New Translation, and Special Studies.* Ktav, 1978. xxxiii/602 pp.

This commentary represents years of research preceded by numerous articles and a full-length book on Job. The author provides a detailed exegesis, textual study, and philological analysis. He also provides forty-two special studies on selected topics. While definitely within the critical tradition, he is moderate and looks at the book as a whole. MS★★⌐

Habel, N. C. *The Book of Job.* OTL. Westminster John Knox/ SCM, 1985. 586 pp.

Habel has produced a major critical commentary on the book of Job. It is a fairly well-rounded commentary, but it concentrates particularly on literary features and theology. While Habel is aware of the questions surrounding the unity of Job, he treats it as a finished whole. MS★★★

Hartley, J. E. *The Book of Job.* NICOT. Eerdmans, 1988. xiv/591 pp.

This is one of the most recent commentaries on Job, and it is a major contribution to the study of the book. This is because it examines all the facets of the book, not necessarily because it is terribly original. It is solidly evangelical in its approach and very well researched. MS★★★★

Janzen, J. G. *Job.* Interp. Westminster John Knox, 1990. viii/273 pp.

In keeping with the parameters of the series, Janzen concentrates on theological significance and contemporary relevance. He does his job admirably, basing his work on an appraisal of such works as Pope and Gordis but often presenting new ideas. He makes a small yet significant shift away from the question "Why do the innocent suffer?" to "Why are the righteous pious?" Very helpful and stimulating. LM★★★

Konkel, A., and T. Longman III. *Job, Ecclesiastes, Song of Songs*. CsBC. Tyndale, 2006. 400 pp.

See also under Ecclesiastes and Song of Songs. Konkel (the author of Job) has excellent technical notes dealing with the meaning of words in the difficult book of Job. His commentary notes are relatively short, though they are extremely thoughtful. LM★★★★

Longman, T., III. *Job*. BCOTWP. Baker Academic, 2012. 496 pp.

It would be inappropriate for me to rate my commentary, but it is an attempt to give a theological explanation that sees the book's main theme as connected to the question of the source of true wisdom. Emphasis is also placed on the place of the book in the canon of the Bible and especially its relationship to the New Testament. LM

Murphy, R. E. *Wisdom Literature: Job, Proverbs, Ruth, Canticles, Ecclesiastes, and Esther*. FOTL. Eerdmans, 1981. 185 pp.

This is the first volume to appear in the FOTL series. Although proportionately shorter than others, it is still full of information and certainly one of the best in the series. Perhaps it is more usable than the others because it is less technical. Murphy is also a very clear writer who is concerned about the meaning of the text. The bibliographies are great (characteristic of the series). S★★★

Pope, M. H. *Job*. AYBC. Yale University Press, 1965. lxxxviii/409 pp.

As with many of the Anchor Yale Bible commentaries, this one's strength is its philological analysis. Pope is one of the very best scholars of Northwest Semitic languages and, unlike Dahood (listed below, under Psalms), is a very sound practitioner of comparative Semitics. This is a solid commentary, but not brilliant like his Song of Songs commentary. MS★★★

Rowley, H. H. *Job*. NCB. Sheffield/Marshall Pickering, 1970. xix/281 pp.

Rowley represents the best of British critical scholarship of the past generation. He was a prolific and knowledgeable writer. He offers thorough discussion of many critical issues and argues for a composite approach to the book of Job. MS★★★

Smick, E. *Job*. REBC 4. Zondervan, 2010. Pp. 675–921.

I helped update this commentary in the second edition and found it very helpful. I did not conform it to my own approach to the book, so I cannot unreservedly recommend it. LM★★★

PSALMS

Allen, L. C. *Psalms 101–150*. 2nd ed. WBC. Nelson/Paternoster, 2002. xxiv/423 pp.

This commentary covers the last third of the Psalter. It is particularly helpful in two areas: language and structure. Allen has very good insight into how the structure of a psalm contributes to its message. While he is good at getting at the message of the psalm in its Old Testament setting, he is very slow in seeing the connection between the text and the New Testament. MS★★⁴

Anderson, A. A. *Psalms*. 2 vols. NCB. Sheffield/Marshall Pickering, 1972. 966 pp.

This is a good modern treatment of the Psalms. It is a little too brief and tied to the restrictive NCB format. The Allen and Craigie volumes are much better. M★★

Briggs, C. A. *Psalms*. 2 vols. ICC. T&T Clark, 1907. cx/422 pp. and viii/572 pp.

This is a highly technical, fairly dated discussion of the Psalms. It is more interesting from the perspective of the history of interpretation than for exposition. S★

Broyles, C. *Psalms*. UBCS. Baker Books, 1999. xvi/539 pp.

This is a brief but solid commentary on the Psalms. One might question, however, how Broyles puts the obvious liturgical nature of the Psalms at odds with their being an expression of individual experience. He recognizes the importance of christological interpretation but does not do much with it. LM★★★★

Craigie, P. C. *Psalms 1–50*. WBC. Nelson/Paternoster, 1983. 375 pp.

This is the first of the three Psalms commentaries in the Word series. As the first in the series, this volume contains introductory material concerning authorship, use, style, and theology. Craigie's commentary is the best of the modern commentaries on the Psalms in matters of language and Old Testament background and message. He is a well-known Ugaritic specialist and is able to cut through the benefits and pitfalls of recent research into the connections between Ugaritic and biblical literature. Two weaknesses of the commentary are his poetical comments and the connections that he draws (or fails to draw) with the New Testament message. This commentary is a must-buy for a serious student of the Psalms, but it should be complemented by a commentary that is strong in its theological insight (like Kidner). MS★★ɔ

Dahood, M. J. *Psalms*. 3 vols. AYBC. Yale University Press, 1965, 1968, 1970. xlvi/329 pp., xxx/399 pp., and liv/490 pp.

Dahood is (in)famous for his use of Northwest Semitic (particularly Ugaritic) in his study of the Psalms. While there is no doubt that cognate languages have helped our understanding of the Psalms, Dahood has overused them in his commentary. There is no methodological control, and even Ugaritic scholars cannot evaluate his arguments. Nonspecialists will be at a total loss. In short, this commentary is very eccentric. S★

Gerstenberger, E. S. *Psalms, Part I: With an Introduction to Cultic Poetry*. FOTL. Eerdmans, 1989. *Psalms, Part 2, and*

Lamentations. FOTL. Eerdmans, 2001. xv/260 pp. and xxii/543 pp.

This is an excellent tool for scholars because of its scholarship and bibliographies. It is extremely doubtful that ministers or laypeople will have much use for this series. Gerstenberger's comments on Lamentations are considerably shorter. S★★★★

Goldingay, J. *Psalms: Psalms 1–41.* BCOTWP. Baker Academic, 2006. *Psalms: Psalms 42–89.* BCOTWP. Baker Academic, 2007. *Psalms: Psalms 90–150.* BCOTWP. Baker Academic, 2008. 640 pp., 744 pp., and 812 pp.

An extensive interpretation of the Psalms, focusing on poetics, grammar, and especially theology of the individual psalms. The best Psalms commentary for the meaning of the book in its original setting, but those looking for a strong discussion of the book's connection with New Testament theology will be disappointed, since the author feels that such a discussion undermines appreciation of the Old Testament itself. LM★★★★↓

Grogan, G. W. *Psalms.* THOTC. Eerdmans, 2008. xi/490 pp.

Grogan is masterful at theological analysis of the book of Psalms. While the treatment of individual psalms is quite brief, the second half of the book provides an illuminating theological analysis of the book as a whole from both an Old Testament and New Testament perspective. LM★★★★★

Hossfeld, F. L., and E. Zenger. *Psalms 2.* Hermeneia. Fortress/SCM, 2005. 580 pp.

The first of three commentaries on the Psalms, Hossfeld and Zenger have chosen to begin with volume 2 that covers Psalms 51–100. They will next publish Psalms 101–150, and then volume 1, which will include an introduction. They rightly believe that they will be in a better position to publish the introduction after working through all the psalms, but perhaps it would have been better, on analogy with the Lord of the Rings movie trilogy, that they publish all three at once! In any case, they have a quite complex understanding of the redaction of the book that leads them to interpret each psalm in light of its neighbors. Let it suffice to say that if one does not agree with their understanding of the redaction and arrangement of the psalms, as I do not, the value of the commentary as a whole is lessened. However, though it would be far from my first choice of commentary on the book, it does provide a number of insights. S★★

Kidner, D. *Psalms 1–72*. TOTC. InterVarsity, 1973. *Psalms 73–150*. TOTC. InterVarsity, 1975. x/257 pp. and vii/235 pp.

Kidner has written two volumes on the Psalms. Unfortunately, they are very brief. This is compensated for by Kidner's ability to write concisely. Thus, in spite of its brevity, this commentary is highly recommended for its theological insight and practical bent. The discussion of the Hebrew text is minimal and is not intended to be very sophisticated. However, the introductory material, particularly the discussion of the meaning of the difficult words in the psalm titles, is very helpful. This commentary is well worth its price. LM★★★

Knight, G. A. F. *Psalms*. 2 vols. DSB. Westminster John Knox, 1982. 350 pp. and 384 pp.

These two volumes, like the others in DSB, are theologically sensitive from a Christian perspective. Knight is moderate in his criticism, devoting more attention to the elucidation of meaning than to other aspects of study, like poetics or the Near Eastern background. LM★★★

Kraus, H.-J. *Psalms 1–59*. CC. Fortress, 1988. *Psalms 60–150*. CC. Fortress, 1993. 559 pp. and 586 pp.

This magisterial work on the Psalms represents the erudition of one of the world's preeminent experts on the Psalms and on the Old Testament for that matter. It is a translation of a German original, the first edition of which was published in 1961; the translation is taken from the fifth edition, published in the late 1970s. The commentary is extremely technical, especially in the introduction. A section-by-section analysis of each psalm is more accessible. Kraus is as interested in theology as he is in poetic forms and *Sitz im Leben*, but this commentary, which clearly comes from the German critical tradition, is only for the extremely serious biblical scholar. S★★★

Mays, J. L. *Psalms*. Interp. Westminster John Knox, 1994. xvii/457 pp.

Mays has given us an exciting new commentary that focuses on the literary expression and theological message of the Psalms. It approaches the Psalms as rich statements of faith in God. The author downplays historical and form-critical approaches. He has a good feel for the Psalms as individual compositions as well as for the structure of the book as a whole. He gives more comment to psalms that have had a bigger impact on later Christian theology. LM★★★★

Tate, M. *Psalms 51–100*. Word, 1990. 579 pp.

This is the third of the Word Psalms volumes to appear, and it is a suitably excellent contribution to the strong commentaries by Allen and Craigie. The one caveat—and it is not insignificant—is that it is weakest in theology of the Psalms. So read John Calvin along with these volumes. MS★★★★

Terrien, S. *The Psalms: Strophic Structure and Theological Commentary*. Eerdmans Critical Commentaries. Eerdmans, 2003. 965 pp.

As the subtitle indicates, Terrien does devote considerable space to determining the strophic structure of each psalm. The results can be helpful, but often are unconvincing. He also provides a short theological essay at the end that is associated with an attempt to date the composition of the psalm, which is always debatable. In short, Terrien's commentary does provide the occasional insight but is a bit idiosyncratic. MS★★

VanGemeren, W. *Psalms*. REBC 5. Zondervan, 2008. 863 pp.

VanGemeren's commentary is excellent on the text and the text's theology and is particularly helpful in sermon preparation. Happily, it is given its own volume. The only downside is his view that the order of the psalms as it presently stands has some kind of theological significance. LM★★★★★

Weiser, A. *The Psalms*. OTL. Westminster John Knox/SCM, 1962. 841 pp.

While not strongly recommended for purchase, this commentary is often theologically insightful. One must be aware of the neoorthodox perspective from which the author is writing and also his belief that all the psalms fit into an annual covenant-renewal ceremony. Weiser is correct to see a close connection between the Psalms and the covenant but mistaken to reconstruct an annual festival with which to connect them. This theory is a definite improvement, however, over Mowinckel's enthronement festival. Weiser is a theological commentator on the Psalms. There is little help in the areas of language or structure. LM★★

Wilcock, M. *The Message of Psalms 1–72*. BST. InterVarsity, 2001. *The Message of Psalms 73–150*. BST. InterVarsity, 2001. 255 pp. and 288 pp.

Short, but very well written, this is a good "starter commentary" for those who are not overly interested in the technical issues but who simply want a solid exposition. L★★★

Wilson, G. H. *Psalms*. Vol. 1. NIVAC. Zondervan/Hodder & Stoughton, 2002. 1024 pp.

Wilson's commentary is strong in all three sections of the series: original meaning, bridging contexts, and contemporary significance. I cannot agree with him about the structure of the book as a whole, which is an original contribution, but the commentary has much value, especially for ministers. LM★★★★★

PROVERBS

Aitken, K. T. *Proverbs*. DSB. Westminster John Knox, 1986.
276 pp.

The introduction to this volume is one of the more critical of
the series, although the bulk of the commentary provides helpful
information. Interestingly, Aitken orders the material in Proverbs
10 and afterward in a topical rather than textual format. LM★★★

Clifford, R. J. *Proverbs*. OTL. Westminster John Knox/SCM,
1999. xvi/286 pp.

This commentary puts more emphasis on text criticism, philology,
and ancient Near Eastern background than some of the other
commentaries listed here. His exposition of the meaning of the
Hebrew is a little less substantial than that of other commentaries,
but it is still very good. MS★★★★

Fox, M. V. *Proverbs 1–9*. AYBC. Yale University Press, 2000.
xix/474 pp.

This is an excellent commentary both because the series allows
more space than other commentaries and because Fox is a master
interpreter. The only drawback is that it covers just the first nine
chapters. Hopefully, we will not have to wait too long for the rest
of the commentary to appear. MS★★★★★

Garrett, D. A. *Proverbs, Ecclesiastes, Song of Songs*. NAC. Broadman, 1993. 448 pp.

See also under Ecclesiastes and Song of Songs. Garrett's introduction is an interesting and helpful conservative approach to the issues
of historical and literary structure. His comments on the text itself
are helpful but too brief. LM★★★

Horine, M. P. *Proverbs and Ecclesiastes*. SHBC. Smyth and
Helwys, 2003. 579 pp.

> The commentary has a pleasing format but not a lot of substance.
> LM★★

Hubbard, D. A. *Proverbs*. ComC. Word, 1989. 487 pp.

> While somewhat more scholarly in tone than other commentaries in
> ComC, Hubbard's contribution is still quite readable and achieves
> the purposes of the series. The introduction, before beginning the
> commentary proper, highlights six principles of interpretation.
> Hubbard gives important guidelines to properly understanding
> the book's forms of speech and literary devices. The section on
> Proverbs 10ff. orders the discussion by topic rather than verse by
> verse. LM★★★★

Kidner, D. *Proverbs*. TOTC. InterVarsity, 1964. 192 pp.

> This small commentary is packed with helpful insight and com-
> ments on the text. It is exegetically sensitive, theologically helpful,
> and orthodox. However, for serious study of Proverbs it should be
> supplemented by a fuller commentary like McKane's. LM★★★★

Longman, T., III. *Proverbs*. BCOTWP. Baker Academic, 2006.
592 pp.

> You can guess my feelings on this commentary. I wouldn't have
> published it if I didn't like it! In this commentary, the focus is on
> the theological and ethical message of the book. Crucial to the
> interpretation of Proverbs is the figure of Woman Wisdom, taken
> as a personification of Yahweh's wisdom and even Yahweh himself.
> Chapters 10–31 are understood to be relatively randomly organized
> bits of advice, prohibitions, encouragements, and warnings. The
> appendix of the commentary contains approximately thirty essays
> synthesizing Proverbs's teaching on such subjects as wealth, family,
> business, ethics, and more. LM

McKane, W. *Proverbs: A New Approach*. OTL. Westminster John Knox/SCM, 1970. xvii/670 pp.

This commentary is a significant contribution to the study of Proverbs, even if the critical conclusions are difficult to appreciate. McKane differentiates the instruction genre of 1–9; 22:17–24:22; and 31:1–9 from the sentence literature of 10–22:16; 24:23–34; and 25–29. However, this commentary is invaluable for the study of the language of Proverbs. The way to use it is to turn to McKane's translation on pages 211–61, where he references his discussion of individual verses. A further debatable conclusion of his study is his division of the sentence literature into three classes. A must for scholarly inquiry into Proverbs, but of doubtful value to the layperson or pastor. MS★★★

Murphy, R. E. *Proverbs*. WBC. Nelson/Paternoster, 1998. lxxiv/306 pp.

Murphy is a preeminent interpreter of Wisdom literature. MS★★★★

Murphy, R. E. *Wisdom Literature: Job, Proverbs, Ruth, Canticles, Ecclesiastes, and Esther*. FOTL. Eerdmans, 1981. 185 pp.

See under Job.

Murphy, R. E., and E. Huwiler. *Proverbs, Ecclesiastes, Song of Songs*. UBCS. Baker Books, 1999. xv/312 pp.

See also under Ecclesiastes and Song of Songs. Murphy, an acknowledged master of the subject, wrote the section on Proverbs, but if one is really interested in his opinions, it is better to get his fuller treatment in the Word series. Perhaps laypeople might find this a more accessible version. LM★★

Perdue, L. G. *Proverbs*. Interp. Westminster John Knox, 2000. xi/289 pp.

This commentary focuses on the literary, structural, ethical, and theological issues of the book of Proverbs. Its perspective is critical but moderately applied—a source of many good insights. LM★★✦

Ross, A. P. *Proverbs*. REBC 6. Zondervan, 2008. Pp. 21–252.

A not-too-exciting, but competent, exposition of the book. Lacks significant theological commentary. The topical index (pp. 38–45) is a helpful guide to finding proverbs on certain topics. LM★★★↵

Scott, R. B. Y. *Proverbs, Ecclesiastes*. AYBC. Yale University Press, 1965. liii/257 pp.

This is not one of the better commentaries in the Anchor series. It represents a classically critical approach to Proverbs. It is not particularly strong in any area of research. S★

Steinmann, A. E. *Proverbs*. ConC. Concordia Publishing House, 2009. xxxix/919 pp.

Steinmann offers a lengthy introduction that considers all the standard issues of date, author, literary form, structure, and text. Of particular note is a consideration of the vocabulary of wisdom. He also pays special attention to matters of gospel and law in the book—not unexpected in a committed Lutheran interpretation. Of benefit is his interest in how Proverbs "promotes Christ," but sometimes he moves too quickly to christological interpretation. LM★★★★

Treier, D. J. *Proverbs and Ecclesiastes*. BTCB. Brazos, 2011. xxvi/256 pp.

This theologically oriented commentary on Proverbs and Ecclesiastes is a stimulating supplement to a more traditional exegetical and biblical-theological commentary. MS★★★↵

van Leeuwen, R. "Proverbs." In *The New Interpreter's Bible*. Vol. 5. Abingdon, 1997. Pp. 19–264.

This commentary exposits the text and also reflects on it theologically. Written from a progressive evangelical perspective, it is one of the best commentaries on Proverbs. LM★★★★

Waltke, B. K. *Proverbs 1–15*. NICOT. Eerdmans, 2004. *Proverbs 16–31*. NICOT. Eerdmans, 2005. 693 pp. and 589 pp.

Waltke's commentary is the product of two decades of reflection and research by this senior scholar. Its length allows him to provide detailed comments on philology and grammar (one of his specialties). He also is theologically sensitive. He argues that the proverbs in chapters 10 and following have a deep structure that affects their interpretation. MS★★★★★

Whybray, R. N. *The Book of Proverbs*. CBC. Cambridge University Press, 1972. x/197 pp.

A good, competent study of the book from a critical perspective. Whybray distinguishes secular from religious proverbs. He studies the book in its ancient Near Eastern setting. LM★★

ECCLESIASTES

Bartholomew, C. *Ecclesiastes*. BCOTWP. Baker Academic, 2009. 448 pp.

Excellent commentary, especially strong in history of interpretation and biblical theology. Bartholomew is very knowledgeable about the history of philosophy as well as modern philosophy and often brings this expertise in play in his exposition of the book. MS★★★★★

Bergant, D. *Job, Ecclesiastes*. OTM. Michael Glazier, 1982. 295 pp.

See under Job.

Brown, W. *Ecclesiastes*. Interp. Westminster John Knox, 2000. xiv/143 pp.

Brown explores the connections between Ecclesiastes and the ancient tale of Gilgamesh, as both examine the significance of life. He believes that the Teacher "offers modern readers the dread and delight of the everyday, the glory of the ordinary." Worth reading. LM★★★

Crenshaw, J. L. *Ecclesiastes*. OTL. Westminster John Knox/SCM, 1987. 192 pp.

Crenshaw's approach may be described as moderately critical. However, this is an excellent commentary. It is not too technical (one gets the feeling that Crenshaw is holding himself back), but it is a profound approach to the book. Highly recommended. MS★★★↙

Davidson, R. *Ecclesiastes and Song of Solomon*. DSB. Westminster John Knox, 1986. viii/160 pp.

See also under Song of Songs. This volume is one of the more critical of the series, especially on such issues as the date and composition of Ecclesiastes. Nonetheless, it provides a helpful and nondogmatic perspective. LM★↙

Eaton, M. A. *Ecclesiastes*. TOTC. InterVarsity, 1983. 159 pp.

Eaton writes well, with a nontechnical audience in mind. He has many good insights into the text, but the commentary is marred by his view that the orthodoxy of Ecclesiastes can be preserved only by turning Qohelet into a "preacher of joy"—quite an exegetical trick. LM★★

Enns, P. E. *Ecclesiastes*. THOTC. Eerdmans, 2011. xiv/238 pp.

"Trust and obey" in spite of suffering and doubt: that is the main message of Ecclesiastes according to Enns. A veteran commentator, Enns carefully and insightfully interprets the book and shows its immense relevance for those of us who today follow the suffering yet victorious Christ. LM★★★★↙

Fox, M. V. *Ecclesiastes*. JPS Bible Commentary. Jewish Publication Society, 2000. xxxviii/87 pp.

The latest of Fox's contributions on Ecclesiastes (and they are many and important) is perhaps the clearest statement of his basic approach to the text. He points out that the book is as close to philosophy as we find in the Hebrew Bible. The book does not try to rationalize the absurdities of life but still affirms God's justice. The commentary also contains a helpful history of interpretation. LM★★★★

Fox, M. V. *A Time to Tear Down and a Time to Build Up: A Rereading of Ecclesiastes*. Eerdmans, 1999. xvii/422 pp. (A substantial revision of *Qohelet and His Contradictions*. Almond, 1989. 384 pp.)

This book may be divided into two parts. The first half treats the book as a whole and offers some tantalizing essays on some key themes, arguing for instance that the key phrase of the book is not "vanity" or "meaninglessness" but rather "absurdity." The second part of the book is a commentary with an emphasis on philology, textual criticism, the book's structure, and interpretation. Fox's idea of Ecclesiastes as a framed monologue is very provocative. MS★★★★

Fredericks, D. C., and D. J. Estes. *Ecclesiastes and the Song of Songs*. AOTC. InterVarsity, 2010. 472 pp.

Fredericks produced the Ecclesiastes portion of this volume. While he provides an intelligent attempt at interpretation, he gets off on a wrong foot in terms of understanding the thematic word *hebel* as "temporary" rather than "meaningless," which influences his whole approach to the book. For Estes's contribution, see under Song of Songs. MS★★↙

Garrett, D. A. *Proverbs, Ecclesiastes, Song of Songs*. NAC. Broadman, 1993. 448 pp.

See also under Proverbs and Song of Songs. Garrett proposes that the main purpose of the book of Ecclesiastes is to impress on its readers that they are moral. He devotes considerable effort to criticizing rival views. The commentary itself is quite short. LM★★

Ginsburg, C. D. *The Song of Songs and Coheleth*. 1857; Ktav, 1970. xliv/528 pp.

Ginsburg was an extremely learned scholar who was well versed in both Christian and Jewish scholarship. His approach is dated, but the prolegomenon, written by S. Blank, attempts to bring certain discussions up-to-date. S★★★

Horine, M. P. *Proverbs and Ecclesiastes*. SHBC. Smyth and Helwys, 2003. 579 pp.

See under Proverbs.

Hubbard, D. A. *Beyond Futility*. Eerdmans, 1976. 128 pp.

This short, lay-oriented commentary is extremely insightful, particularly in its comments on how Christ moves beyond the futility of Qohelet. LM★★★

Kaiser, W. C., Jr. *Ecclesiastes: Total Life*. Moody, 1979. 128 pp.

Kaiser has written a very readable commentary on the book of Ecclesiastes. Unfortunately, he takes an untenable approach to the book, turning the main speaker Qohelet into an orthodox "preacher of joy." LM★★

Kidner, D. *The Message of Ecclesiastes: A Time to Mourn and a Time to Dance*. BST. InterVarsity, 1976. 110 pp.

This commentary is well written and sensible in its approach to Ecclesiastes. Shows application to life as well. LM★★★

Konkel, A., and T. Longman III. *Job, Ecclesiastes, Song of Songs*. CsBC. Tyndale, 2006. 400 pp.

See also under Job and Song of Songs. I authored the Ecclesiastes and Song of Songs commentaries. The commentary on Ecclesiastes views the Teacher as someone who thinks about the meaning of life in the context of a fallen world and comes up empty. His words are framed by a second wise man who is teaching his son to avoid such an approach to life. LM

Kruger, T. *Qoheleth*. Hermeneia. Fortress/SCM, 2004. 320 pp.

Kruger argues that the book of Ecclesiastes promotes eating, drinking, and pleasure as the "highest good," especially in the light of the meaninglessness of other potential avenues of significance. He situates this message in the late third century BC and in relationship to contemporary Greek philosophy. S★★★

Lohfink, N. *Qoheleth*. CC. Fortress, 2003. 176 pp.

Lohfink argues that Ecclesiastes disputes not just the wisdom of Proverbs but also Hellenistic wisdom. It mediates Hellenistic philosophy to Jews in a way that will help them without requiring them to abandon their Judaism. He dates the book to the third century BC. MS★↵

Longman, T., III. *Ecclesiastes*. NICOT. Eerdmans, 1998. xvi/306 pp.

This commentary deals with the philology (providing a new translation), literary character, and theological message of the book. I argue that the author is not Solomon, but that Ecclesiastes adopts a Solomonic persona to show the meaninglessness of life. Takes a canonical-christocentric approach to the meaning of the book. MS

Murphy, R. E. *Ecclesiastes*. WBC. Nelson/Paternoster, 1992. 254 pp.

Murphy is one of the preeminent interpreters of wisdom, and serious students of Ecclesiastes will read this commentary carefully. He is particularly interesting to read for his translation and exegetical notes. However, there are better commentaries to get at the original meaning and theological significance of Ecclesiastes. MS★★↵

Murphy, R. E. *Wisdom Literature: Job, Proverbs, Ruth, Canticles, Ecclesiastes, and Esther*. FOTL. Eerdmans, 1981. 185 pp.

See under Job.

Murphy, R. E., and E. Huwiler. *Proverbs, Ecclesiastes, Song of Songs*. UBCS. Baker Books, 1999. xv/312 pp.

See also under Proverbs and Song of Songs. Huwiler produced the interpretation of Ecclesiastes here. She makes a fundamental error in not differentiating the theology of Qohelet from that of the book as a whole. She basically sees the book as affirming the struggle of postmodernism. LM★★

Provan, I. *Ecclesiastes/Song of Songs*. NIVAC. Zondervan/Hodder & Stoughton, 2001. 399 pp.

Provan has written one of the most interesting commentaries on these two intriguing books. Even though one may not agree with his final conclusions, his thinking is provocative and will lead the reader to think through old issues. One example is his understanding of the Song as a drama having three main characters. The basic plot as he reconstructs it is that Solomon has forced a country girl into his harem, though she continues to love the shepherd boy back home. The theme of the book proclaims that true love resists coerced legal love. LM★★★★

Scott, R. B. Y. *Proverbs, Ecclesiastes*. AYBC. Yale University Press, 1965. liii/257 pp.

See also under Proverbs. Ecclesiastes is treated very briefly, almost like an afterthought. S★

Seow, C.-L. *Ecclesiastes*. AYBC. Yale University Press, 1997. xxiv/419 pp.

This readable yet scholarly commentary argues for a specific date of the book in the Persian period. While this argument is not compelling, the theological notes are often insightful. MS★★★★

Shepherd, J. E. *Ecclesiastes.* REBC 6. Zondervan, 2008.
Pp. 253–365.

An interesting and helpful short commentary on the book. Most notable is his attempt to identify "the Teacher" (Qohelet) with Hezekiah. Very readable. LM★★★★

Treier, D. J. *Proverbs and Ecclesiastes.* BTCB. Brazos, 2011.
xxvi/256 pp.

See under Proverbs.

Whybray, R. N. *Ecclesiastes.* NCB. Sheffield/Marshall Pickering, 1989. xxiii/179 pp.

Whybray, a prolific and respected English Old Testament scholar, has written on Ecclesiastes before, most notably in his article "Qohelet: Preacher of Joy" (*Journal for the Study of the Old Testament* 23 [1982]: 87–98). Here, as there, he leans toward an interpretation that sees Qohelet as a realist who, in spite of clearly seeing all the problems of a world living under the effects of the curse, nonetheless believes that God wants people to enjoy life. Whybray argues that Ecclesiastes is late (third century BC) and under some Greek influence. MS★★★

SONG OF SONGS

Carr, G. L. *Song of Songs.* TOTC. InterVarsity, 1984. 175 pp.

This is a good popular exposition of the Song. Much scholarly research stands behind it. Carr takes a flexible approach to authorship and makes an adequate presentation of alternative approaches to the book. He himself advocates a "natural reading." LM★★★

Davidson, R. *Ecclesiastes and Song of Solomon*. DSB. Westminster John Knox, 1986. viii/160 pp.

See also under Ecclesiastes. Davidson rightly takes the view that the Song is a collection of love poems. He gives a helpful analysis of the imagery of the book. LM★★★

Exum, C. J. *Song of Songs*. OTL. Westminster John Knox/SCM, 2005. xxiii/263 pp.

The Song is a collection of lyric poems but has a kind of unity or progression of sorts as the poems express a pattern of longing leading to satisfaction leading to renewed longing. The introduction has an interesting account of feminist and queer readings of the Song. MS★★★★

Fredericks, D. C., and D. J. Estes. *Ecclesiastes and the Song of Songs*. AOTC. InterVarsity, 2010. 472 pp.

Estes wrote the Song of Songs commentary in this volume. He takes a similar approach to the Song as my commentary (below) in seeing it as an anthology of love poems rather than as a drama. He recognizes that the Man and the Woman are not actual people, but still calls them Solomon and Shulammith throughout, pointing out that these names are both built on a root related to the Hebrew word *shalom* ("contented"). For Fredericks's contribution, see under Ecclesiastes. MS★★★★

Garrett, D. A. *Proverbs, Ecclesiastes, Song of Songs*. NAC. Broadman, 1993. 448 pp.

See also under Proverbs and Ecclesiastes. Garrett advocates the Solomonic authorship of the book. He treats the Song as a unified love poem and writes that it is neither an allegory nor a drama. LM★★

Garrett, D. A., and P. R. House. *Song of Songs/Lamentations.* WBC. Nelson/Paternoster, 2004. 479 pp.

See also under Lamentations. Garrett wrote the commentary on the Song of Songs. This is a more scholarly version of the NAC commentary. He treats the book as lyric poetry, a unified work with a chiastic structure composed of 13 songs (or cantos). He describes the man and woman as the tenor and soprano to underline his belief that this was a musical production. He believes that the songs have a progression in telling the story of the sexual coming-of-age of a young woman. In part, he takes a structuralist approach as he views it as a heroic quest on the part of the woman as she moves from the status of virgin to nonvirgin. S★★✦

Gledhill, T. *The Message of the Song of Songs: The Lyrics of Love.* BST. InterVarsity, 1994. 254 pp.

This is a model popular commentary. It is well written, easy to read, yet profound. Also, Gledhill has an excellent literary sense; he neither simply adopts traditional readings nor gives in to the excesses of contemporary psychological readings of the text. LM★★★★

Griffiths, P. J. *Song of Songs.* BTCB. Brazos, 2011. 182 pp.

Professor of Catholic theology at Duke Divinity School, Griffiths provides a perspective not found in other commentaries. He comments on the Latin Version of the Song since he does not believe there is one original text. Since I am one of those who does give priority to the Masoretic version of the Song, I can't recommend this commentary for typical use. The introduction is interesting reading to get insight into a prominent Catholic theologian's view of Scripture. He adopts an allegorical approach that sees the man as God and the woman as Israel-Church-Mary-individual Christian. MS★★

Hess, R. S. *Song of Songs.* BCOTWP. Baker Academic, 2005. 285 pp.

Hess provides a detailed analysis of this book of Old Testament love poetry. He provides excellent philological analysis and shows keen poetic sensibility. He is an expert in ancient Near Eastern background and also provides very helpful theological comments on the book. MS★★★⭑

Jenson, R. W. *Song of Songs*. Interp. Westminster John Knox, 2004. x/106 pp.

Jenson is a theologian, not a biblical scholar, but he has interpretive sensitivity and sophistication. He believes that "the Song is a structured suite of poems building to an emotional climax" (4) and that while on one level it does speak of human sexuality, on another level (either that of the text itself or on the canonical level) it is appropriate to read it allegorically as the love between God and his people. Though I would not use allegory to describe his reading since that usually denotes early interpreters' fanciful handling of the details of the text, I affirm the principle that the canonical text does concern divine-human relationships. MS★★★★

Keel, O. *The Song of Songs*. CC. Fortress, 1994. ix/308 pp.

Keel demonstrates excellent literary and overall exegetical sensibilities. He even makes some insightful theological comments. The translation and writing are excellent, even humorous at times. A special feature, not unusual to Keel's work, is the presence of copies of relevant Near Eastern art. SM★★★★

Konkel, A., and T. Longman III. *Job, Ecclesiastes, Song of Songs*. CsBC. Tyndale, 2006. 400 pp.

See also under Job and Ecclesiastes. I authored the Ecclesiastes and Song of Songs commentaries. I approach the Song of Songs as containing twenty-three love poems that celebrate love and occasionally warn about its dangers. LM

Longman, T., III. *Song of Songs*. NICOT. Eerdmans, 2001. xvi/238 pp.

My commentary on the Song has a relatively lengthy introduction discussing such pivotal interpretive issues as genre and ancient

Near Eastern background as well as the controversial subject of authorship. The Song is understood to be an anthology of twenty-three love poems. The theological significance of the book is fully discussed. MS

Mitchell, C. W. *Song of Songs*. ConC. Concordia Publishing House, 2003. xliii/1230 pp.

As the page length indicates, this is quite a full commentary! In keeping with the series, this book is distinctively Lutheran in its interpretation with a strong interest in law-gospel and in "what promotes Christ" in the book. It does not ignore the implications of the book for marriage but puts all the emphasis on a christological reading. LM★★★✓

Murphy, R. E. *The Song of Songs*. Hermeneia. Fortress/SCM, 1990. xxii/227 pp.

Murphy provides an excellent critical reading of the text. He emphasizes its final form and is concerned with theological issues. His lengthy introduction gives a helpful survey of the history of interpretation, issues of prosody, and basic interpretive approach. MS★★★★

Murphy, R. E. *Wisdom Literature: Job, Proverbs, Ruth, Canticles, Ecclesiastes, and Esther*. FOTL. Eerdmans, 1981. 185 pp.

See under Job.

Murphy, R. E., and E. Huwiler. *Proverbs, Ecclesiastes, Song of Songs*. UBCS. Baker Books, 1999. xv/312 pp.

See also under Proverbs and Ecclesiastes. Huwiler's analysis of the Song of Songs is much better than her treatment of Ecclesiastes. LM★★★

Pope, M. H. *Song of Songs*. AYBC. Yale University Press, 1977. xxi/743 pp.

This commentary contains a wealth of linguistic, literary, and historical information. The history of interpretation, comparative sections, and fifty-five-page bibliography are worth the price of the book. Pope fairly represents positions different from his own. His overall approach to the book as connected with the love and death cults of the ancient world leaves much to be desired but is interesting. MS★★★★

Provan, I. *Ecclesiastes/Song of Songs*. NIVAC. Zondervan/Hodder & Stoughton, 2001. 399 pp.

See under Ecclesiastes.

Schwab, G. M. *Song of Songs*. REBC 6. Zondervan, 2008. Pp. 366–431.

Schwab combines the skills of an exegete with that of a person sensitive to issues of sexuality, helpful for the study of this sensuous love poem. He is to be commended for reading the Song as a collection of love poems rather than as a drama. He navigates the book's theological meaning very well. LM★★★★✔

Snaith, J. G. *Song of Songs*. NCB. Sheffield/Marshall Pickering, 1993. 140 pp.

Insights can be found here and there, but it is really too brief to compete with the other commentaries available. LM★★

ISAIAH

Baltzer, K. *Deutero-Isaiah: A Commentary on Isaiah 40–55*. Hermeneia. Fortress/SCM, 2001. 400 pp.

Baltzer treats Deutero-Isaiah as a six-act liturgical drama that was performed during Passover/Mazzot. Hymns mark the end of acts. He dates this material later than even traditional historical criticism (450–400 BC). Scholars will need to consult this commentary. S★★★

Blenkinsopp, J. *Isaiah 1–39.* AYBC. Yale University Press, 2000. *Isaiah 40–55.* AYBC. Yale University Press, 2002. *Isaiah 56–66.* AYBC. Yale University Press, 2003. xix/525 pp., xvii/411 pp., and xvi/348 pp.

Blenkinsopp takes a synchronic and diachronic approach to the book, but it is hard to see the former for the latter. Contrary to the current trend that it is virtually impossible to get to authentic eighth-century Isaiah, even in chapters 1–39, he does hold that there is a substratum of such material, though he believes "the eighth-century B.C.E. prophet has been buried under an exegetical mountain" (*Isaiah 1–39*, 90). All three volumes have lengthy and informative introductions as well as extensive bibliographies. S★★★

Childs, B. S. *Isaiah.* OTL. Westminster John Knox/SCM, 2001. xx/555 pp.

Well worth getting is Childs's canon-conscious take on the book. Though not quite as well done in depth and detail as his much earlier Exodus commentary, it is helpful to see how he manages what he considers to be the compositional history of the book with the final form's theological message. MS★★★★

Clements, R. E. *Isaiah 1–39.* NCB. Sheffield, 1980. xvi/301 pp.

Clements is an evangelical who practices a moderate higher criticism. He is one of the most prolific British writers in the field of Old Testament. He has a good writing style and practices sensitive exegesis. However, his critical perspective mars many of his insights. MS★★★

Goldingay, J. *Isaiah.* UBCS. Baker Books, 2001. x/397 pp.

Goldingay presents a very readable and insightful interpretation of Isaiah in a compact format. Some readers will not like his approach to the history of the book's composition, which he attributes not only to the prophet (whom he calls the Ambassador), but to others whom he terms the Disciple, the Poet, and the Preacher. It would be a great mistake for people put off by these conclusions to ignore this important commentary. Only its brevity keeps it from being a five-star commentary. MS★★★★

Grogan, G. W. *Isaiah*. REBC 6. Zondervan, 2008. Pp. 432–863.

Grogan has produced one of the best short commentaries on the prophet Isaiah. He is particularly adept at bringing out the theological meaning of the book. While he presents a strong argument in favor of the authorial unity of the book, he does not write off some who, while accepting the idea of supernatural prophecy, opt for multiple authorship. LM★★★★ʲ

Hanson, P. D. *Isaiah 40–66*. Interp. Westminster John Knox, 1995. 255 pp.

Hanson's volume complements Seitz's commentary (listed below) by treating "Second" Isaiah. Like Seitz, Hanson takes a moderately critical stance, arguing that, though there are many literary and theological connections throughout the book as a whole, these chapters come from a hand other than the eighth-century prophet. It is a work from the exilic and early exilic periods. Though this historical conclusion will disappoint more conservative readers, it should not keep them from appreciating the fine theological analysis of the book. M★★★★

Kaiser, O. *Isaiah 1–39*. 2 vols. OTL. Westminster John Knox/ SCM, 1972. xx/170 pp. and xix/412 pp.

Kaiser represents the best of German critical scholarship on the book of Isaiah. S★★★

Knight, G. A. F. *Isaiah 40–55: Servant Theology.* ITC. Handsel, 1984. *Isaiah 56–66: The New Israel.* ITC. Handsel, 1985. ix/204 pp. and xvii/126 pp.

Although he argues against an eighth-century date for the prophecy, Knight brackets historical-critical concerns. He shows great sensitivity to exegetical and theological issues. LM★★★

McKenzie, J. L. *Second Isaiah.* AYBC. Yale University Press, 1968. lxxi/225 pp.

Although its title might lead the reader to think otherwise, McKenzie actually comments on both what he calls Second Isaiah and Third Isaiah. The latter he thinks is made up of miscellaneous oracles from anonymous sources. There are better commentaries on the subject, in both the critical and evangelical camps. S★★

Motyer, J. A. *Isaiah.* TOTC. InterVarsity, 1999. 408 pp.

Though the approach to the book is substantially the same as his longer and more technical commentary (listed below), the present volume is more accessible to laypeople. Motyer and Oswalt provide the most lucid exposition of Isaiah from a traditional viewpoint that sees the whole book as coming largely from the eighth century. LM★★★★

Motyer, J. A. *The Prophecy of Isaiah: An Introduction and Commentary.* InterVarsity, 1994. 544 pp.

This commentary represents three decades of work by the author on the biblical book. It is thoroughly researched and thought-out. It represents the best of a conservative evangelical approach to the book at the end of the twentieth century. It is best in theological matters. MS★★★★

Oswalt, J. N. *Isaiah.* NIVAC. Zondervan/Hodder & Stoughton, 2003. 736 pp.

Oswalt provides a commendable scholarly study of Isaiah in the NIVAC series. This volume presents the original meaning of Isaiah

in a more accessible manner and also provides a powerful account-
ing of the continuing relevance of this "prince of the prophets"
(17). Oswalt shows himself to be not only a sensitive exegete but
also a sensitive pastor in this volume. LM★★★★★

Oswalt, J. N. *Isaiah 1–39*. NICOT. Eerdmans, 1986. *Isaiah 40–66*.
NICOT. Eerdmans, 1998. xiii/746 pp. and xviii/755 pp.

These volumes are solidly conservative and well researched. MS★★★★

Ridderbos, J. *Isaiah*. BSC. Zondervan, 1985. 580 pp.

This commentary is a translation of a Dutch original first published
in 1950/51. It is oriented toward the minister. Ridderbos is a top-
flight scholar. He accepts the essential unity of Isaiah, although
admitting some secondary glosses added by Isaiah's disciples. The
commentary has the advantages and disadvantages of a one-volume
commentary on such a long and complex biblical book. It is easy
to digest but often superficial (largely due to length constraints).
It is written from a Reformed, conservative perspective. MS★★★

Sawyer, J. F. A. *Isaiah*. 2 vols. DSB. Westminster John Knox, 1984,
1986. 280 pp. and 240 pp.

Sawyer accepts the common critical understanding of Isaiah as having been composed by different individuals inspired by the original
eighth-century prophet. In the commentary proper, however, he
does not deal with such historical issues; rather, he concentrates
on the meaning of the text for today. LM★★★

Seitz, C. R. *Isaiah 1–39*. Interp. Westminster John Knox, 1993.
xvi/271 pp.

This very readable commentary presents the best moderately critical
approach to the book of Isaiah. Literary context takes the fore in
Seitz's interpretation of Isaiah's oracles. He does not bypass the
historical setting, though it is here that evangelicals will have the
most difficulty. MS★★★★

Sweeney, M. A. *Isaiah 1–39 with an Introduction to Prophetic Literature*. FOTL. Eerdmans, 1996. xix/547 pp.

For those who want an up-to-date, learned, and well-written introduction to the form criticism of Isaiah this is the best source. In keeping with the series, the issues and discussion are too technical for lay readers, and conservative readers will not like some of his conclusions, but this is an excellent piece of work. S★★★★★

Walker, L. L., and E. A. Martens. *Isaiah, Jeremiah, Lamentations*. CsBC. Tyndale, 2005. 593 pp.

See also under Jeremiah. Walker wrote the Isaiah commentary. It is a good, solid interpretation of the text based on the New Living Translation. It represents a thoughtful, conservative approach to the text. Handy for those who want a brief exposition, but for those who want something more substantial from a similar perspective, see Oswalt's two contributions. LM★★★

Watts, J. D. W. *Isaiah*. 2 vols. WBC. Nelson/Paternoster, 1985, 1987. lvii/449 pp. and xxiii/385 pp.

Watts has written a commentary on the canonical form of the book. He is not concerned with prehistory but interprets the book in its present form. This form points to a fifth-century date for the book, although the author used materials from earlier (eighth-century) settings. Watts proposes a twelvefold structure to the book (in two parts [chaps. 1–39; 40–66]) that follows a kind of chronological flow. (Reviewers question his approach here.) This is an interesting and provocative commentary. MS★★★

Westermann, C. *Isaiah 40–66*. OTL. Westminster John Knox/ SCM, 1969. iv/429 pp.

This volume completes Kaiser's first two volumes in the OTL series. Westermann here offers a commentary on what he calls Deutero- and Trito-Isaiah. Westermann is always insightful, and this commentary should not be ignored because of its critical basis. MS★★★★

Whybray, R. N. *Isaiah 40–66.* NCB. Sheffield/Marshall Pickering, 1980. 301 pp.

Whybray divides his commentary between chapters 40–55 (Deutero-Isaiah) and 56–66 (Trito-Isaiah). He carefully describes the historical background of Deutero-Isaiah in the neo-Babylonian period. He applies the form-critical method to the elucidation of the text. His exposition is clear and scholarly, which is what we expect from Whybray. The format of the series, however, is very restricting. LM★★★

Wildberger, H. *Isaiah 1–12.* CC. Fortress, 1991. *Isaiah 13–27.* CC. Fortress, 1997. *Isaiah 28–39.* CC. Fortress, 2002. x/524 pp., x/624 pp., and 720 pp.

This detailed, close reading of the book of Isaiah covers most of the main avenues of research into a biblical book: text, source, form, theology, and so forth. It is from a critical perspective. The bibliographies are extensive. S★★★★

Young, E. J. *The Book of Isaiah.* 3 vols. Eerdmans, 1965, 1969, 1972. xii/534 pp., 604 pp., and 579 pp.

Young's commentary was originally in the NICOT series, but the series floundered after his work came out and has only been revived in the past decade (without Young's commentary; see Oswalt). Young was a meticulous and detailed scholar, which is evident in his work here. He is a better philologist than literary scholar or biblical theologian, but the commentary is well worth the money. The commentary takes a very conservative approach to Isaiah. Young's writing style is tedious. MS★★

JEREMIAH

Allen, L. C. *Jeremiah*. OTL. Westminster John Knox, 2008. xxix/546 pp.

Allen is an excellent scholar and does a great job articulating the message of Jeremiah in its original context. He helpfully puts his focus on the final form of the book. He pays little attention to the book from a New Testament perspective, I assume by design (there is even only a very brief mention of New Testament's appropriation of the New Covenant [see 31:31–34]). MS★★★★

Boadt, L. *Jeremiah 1–25*. OTM. Michael Glazier, 1982. *Jeremiah 26–52, Habakkuk, Zephaniah, Nahum*. OTM. Michael Glazier, 1982. xxviii/213 pp. and xii/276 pp.

A popular two-volume theological commentary on four prophets from the latter half of the seventh century. Boadt treats them together because they offer different perspectives on the same historical events. LM★★★

Bright, J. *Jeremiah*. AYBC. Yale University Press, 1965. cxliv/372 pp.

This is one of the better commentaries on Jeremiah, although it is written from a moderately critical angle. Bright has good theological and literary sense. One disconcerting feature of this commentary is its arrangement. Bright has chosen to depart from Jeremiah's more topical arrangement and has commented on the text in a reconstructed chronological order. MS★★★

Brown, M. L. *Jeremiah*. REBC 7. Zondervan, 2010. Pp. 21–572.

A substantial and intelligent commentary. Brown is well acquainted with not only modern scholarship on the book but also rabbinic commentary, and he uses both to help him understand the prophet. LM★★★★

Brueggemann, W. *Jeremiah 1–25: To Pluck Up, to Tear Down.* ITC. Handsel, 1988. *Jeremiah 26–52: To Build, to Plant.* ITC. Handsel, 1991. x/289 pp. and xi/298 pp. [Also available as *A Commentary on Jeremiah: Exile and Homecoming.* Eerdmans, 1998. xiv/502 pp.]

Brueggemann provides an easy-to-read and contemporary interpretation of the book of Jeremiah. As usual, he is thought-provoking in his reading. LM★★★★

Carroll, R. P. *The Book of Jeremiah.* OTL. Westminster John Knox/SCM, 1986. 874 pp.

Carroll includes an excellent bibliography. His commentary emphasizes a redaction-critical approach to the book in an attempt to reconcile what he calls the "disparate *personae* of Jeremiah represented by the various levels of tradition in it" (37). S★★

Clements, R. E. *Jeremiah.* Interp. Westminster John Knox, 1988. xi/276 pp.

Clements adopts a moderately critical approach to questions of composition and authorship. He concentrates on integrating historical background and theological message. The book is clearly written and profitable. LM★★★

Craigie, P. C., P. H. Kelley, and J. F. Drinkard Jr. *Jeremiah 1–25.* WBC. Nelson/Paternoster, 1991. xlvii/389 pp.

Craigie died in a car accident after finishing only the first seven chapters in this commentary. Kelley and Drinkard combined to finish this volume; G. Keown is the author of the second volume on Jeremiah. The volume as a whole is consistent with Craigie's high level of scholarship. The volume is especially helpful in matters of language and form. The analysis of content is a little thin, and theological reflection is at a minimum. The volume's bibliographies are extensive. MS★★↲

Davidson, R. *Jeremiah and Lamentations.* 2 vols. DSB. Westminster John Knox, 1983, 1985. 180 pp. and 228 pp.

See also under Lamentations. Davidson devotes all of the first volume and most of the second to a study of the prophecy of Jeremiah. While he accepts a moderately critical approach to the text, he does not present critical discussions in the commentary. The result is a popularly written and helpful exposition. LM★★✦

Dearman, J. A. *Jeremiah/Lamentations.* NIVAC. Zondervan/Hodder & Stoughton, 2002. 488 pp.

A very sensitive theological reading that also brings these two books into touch with the contemporary world. In keeping with the series, Dearman does not deal with technical issues. LM★★★★

Fretheim, T. E. *Jeremiah.* SHBC. Smyth and Helwys, 2002. 684 pp.

This is an extremely well-written commentary with an emphasis on Jeremiah as literature and theology, though there is attention to critical issues and history as well. Fretheim's approach will appeal to both conservative and critically minded readers. Highly recommended. LM★★★★★

Harrison, R. K. *Jeremiah and Lamentations.* TOTC. InterVarsity, 1973. 240 pp.

Due to its size restrictions, this commentary is unable to compare with some of the others as a major research tool. However, it is an excellent commentary for laypeople. The emphasis is on history, philology, and theology. LM★★★

Holladay, W. L. *Jeremiah.* 2 vols. Hermeneia. Fortress/SCM, 1986, 1989. xxii/682 pp. and xxxi/543 pp.

This is a major contribution to Jeremiah studies written from a form-critical perspective; it should be consulted by everyone who does serious work on the book. Like the others in the series, it is a well-presented commentary. MS★★★★

Huey, F. B., Jr. *Jeremiah, Lamentations*. NAC. Broadman, 1993. 512 pp.

This commentary, in keeping with the series, emphasizes the theological message of the book in its historical context. What it says is true and helpful, as far as it goes, and that is its main shortcoming. It is rather thin. Huey represents a traditional conservative approach to the books that he studies. LM★★

Jones, D. R. *Jeremiah*. NCB. Sheffield/Marshall Pickering, 1992. 557 pp.

This commentary produced by a competent senior scholar has a higher level of confidence in the history of the book than most critics. He gives a strong synchronic exposition, but, due to the constraints of the series, the analysis is not detailed. LM★★★

Keown, G. L., P. J. Scalise, and T. G. Smothers. *Jeremiah 26–52*. WBC. Nelson/Paternoster, 1995. 402 pp.

When Peter Craigie, the original contributor to the Word series on Jeremiah, died, it was an odd decision to assign the rest of the book to five other scholars (including Kelley and Drinkard in vol. 1). MS★★★

Longman, T., III. *Jeremiah, Lamentations*. UBCS. Baker Books, 2008. xvi/412 pp.

See also under Lamentations. My intention in this short commentary on the longest book in the Bible is to give a concise interpretation of each unit of the book with an emphasis on its theological message. I highlight in particular the importance of covenant to Jeremiah. There are some technical notes on particularly troublesome passages. LM

Lundbom, J. R. *Jeremiah 1–20*. AYBC. Yale University Press, 1999. *Jeremiah 21–36*. AYBC. Yale University Press, 2004. *Jeremiah 37–52*. AYBC. Yale University Press, 2004. 934 pp., 649 pp., and 624 pp.

This is a brilliant commentary on the book in its original meaning, though Lundbom is not interested in Jeremiah's theology. A must-buy for those ministers and scholars who are really interested in looking at the book. MS★★★★★

McKane, W. *A Critical and Exegetical Commentary on Jeremiah*. 2 vols. ICC. T&T Clark, 1986, 1996. cxxii/658 pp. and clxxiv/785 pp.

This is an example of the "new generation" ICC commentaries. Not many Old Testament commentaries are out yet. The new commentaries have the same critical concerns as the older series: textual criticism, philology, and historical matters. There is little theological reflection. However, since the newer volumes take into account recent advances in scholarship, these volumes are more valuable than the older ones. McKane's volumes have extensive text-critical and redaction-critical discussions. A must for all scholars, it is just as well ignored by most laypersons and ministers. S★★★

Thompson, J. A. *The Book of Jeremiah*. NICOT. Eerdmans, 1979. xii/819 pp.

Thompson takes a more traditional and evangelical approach to the book. However, he does allow for some non-Jeremiah parts. He treats Jeremiah as a real person in a definite historical setting. Well worth getting. MS★★✔

Walker, L. L., and E. A. Martens. *Isaiah, Jeremiah, Lamentations*. CsBC. Tyndale, 2005. 593 pp.

Martens provides a readable and helpful exposition of Jeremiah and Lamentations, two books on which he is an expert. His strength is biblical theology. LM★★★★

LAMENTATIONS

Berlin, A. *Lamentations: A Commentary*. OTL. Westminster John Knox/SCM, 2002. xxvi/135 pp.

Berlin devotes a large part of this relatively short commentary to the introduction. Though short, her work contains much substance and insight. She focuses on literary features, particularly the book's metaphors, to get at the theology of the book. She lists "purity, mourning, repentance, and the Davidic covenant" (ix) as particularly important themes in the book. She has an admirable agnosticism concerning historical-critical issues and studies the book in relation to the background of other ancient Near Eastern literature. MS★★★★★

Davidson, R. *Jeremiah and Lamentations*. Vol. 2. DSB. Westminster John Knox, 1985. 228 pp.

See also under Jeremiah. Davidson's comments on Lamentations are vivid and concise. He uses a number of modern analogies to bring the horror of the destruction of Jerusalem to life. LM★★⌡

Dearman, J. A. *Jeremiah/Lamentations*. NIVAC. Zondervan/Hodder & Stoughton, 2002. 488 pp.

See under Jeremiah.

Dobbs-Allsopp, F. W. *Lamentations*. Interp. Westminster John Knox, 2002. xiv/159 pp.

Dobbs-Allsopp gives a very sensitive theological and existential interpretation of the book. This commentary is especially helpful to those who preach and want to bridge from Lamentations to the contemporary situation. LM★★★⌡

Ferris, P. W. *Lamentations.* REBC 7. Zondervan, 2010.
Pp. 573–640.

Ferris is a longtime student of city laments in the ancient Near
East and the book of Lamentations in particular. He utilizes his
lengthy study well in expositing this short but important biblical
book. LM★★★★

Garrett, D. A., and P. R. House. *Song of Songs/Lamentations.*
WBC. Nelson/Paternoster, 2004. 479 pp.

See also under Song of Songs. House wrote the commentary on
Lamentations. He does an excellent job of building on the insights
of such previous scholars as Albrektson, Gottwald, and Renkema.
He has an appreciative but helpfully critical interaction with schol-
ars like Dobbs-Allsopp who believe that Lamentations presents
God as an abuser or bully. MS★★★★

Gerstenberger, E. S. *Psalms, Part 2, and Lamentations.* FOTL.
Eerdmans, 2001. xxii/543 pp.

See under Psalms.

Harrison, R. K. *Jeremiah and Lamentations.* TOTC. InterVarsity,
1973. 240 pp.

See under Jeremiah.

Hillers, D. R. *Lamentations.* 2nd ed. AYBC. Yale University Press,
1992. xiv/175 pp.

A good commentary. It does a good job elucidating the book's
Near Eastern literary background. MS★★★

Huey, F. B., Jr. *Jeremiah, Lamentations.* NAC. Broadman, 1993.
512 pp.

See under Jeremiah.

Longman, T., III. *Jeremiah, Lamentations*. UBCS. Baker Books, 2008. xvi/412 pp.

See also under Jeremiah. My intention in this short commentary is to give a concise interpretation of each unit of the book with an emphasis on its theological message. There are some technical notes on particularly troublesome passages. I also try to counter the recent tendency to downplay the book's acknowledgment of Israel's sin as an explanation for its suffering, though acknowledging that the poet attempts to convince God that Israel has been punished enough. LM

Parry, R. A. *Lamentations*. THOTC. Eerdmans, 2010. xii/260 pp.

Parry gives us a wonderful theological reflection on the book of Lamentations, both in its Old Testament setting as well as from a New Testament perspective. A wonderful resource for preachers. LM★★★★★

Provan, I. *Lamentations*. NCB. Sheffield/Marshall Pickering, 1991. 134 pp.

The author provides clearly written and cogent discussions of the book's difficulties, though I think he may be a bit overly skeptical in pinning down the book's historical setting. He understands the book to be "man's struggle to speak in the face of God's silence." LM★★★★★

Walker, L. L., and E. A Martens. *Isaiah, Jeremiah, Lamentations*. CsBC. Tyndale, 2005. 593 pp.

See under Jeremiah.

EZEKIEL

Alexander, R. H. *Ezekiel*. REBC 7. Zondervan, 2010. Pp. 641–924.

A concise and often-insightful commentary. Occasionally the author reveals his dispensationalist interpretive stance. LM★★★

Allen, L. C. *Ezekiel 1–19*. WBC. Nelson/Paternoster, 1994. *Ezekiel 20–48*. WBC. Nelson/Paternoster, 1990. 342 pp. and xxviii/301 pp.

Brownlee's death interrupted the completion of his commentary on Ezekiel. Allen now has completed his work. Brownlee's approach was somewhat eccentric, and Allen departs from it and goes his own way. While this divergence is unfortunate, it may be the best for the series. Allen is concerned with both the final form of the book as well as its composition. In this regard, he sees himself mediating the positions represented by Greenberg and Zimmerli. MS★★★★

Blenkinsopp, J. *Ezekiel*. Interp. Westminster John Knox, 1990. vi/242 pp.

This series, written from a moderately critical perspective, is a delight to read. It is rich in theological insight and very accessible. Blenkinsopp's commentary is no exception. In the introduction, he clearly explains his view of how a prophetic book grows and applies it to Ezekiel. He focuses on religious and theological issues, with a special concentration on the presence/absence of God. LM★★★★

Block, D. I. *The Book of Ezekiel 1–24*. NICOT. Eerdmans, 1997. *The Book of Ezekiel 25–48*. NICOT. Eerdmans, 1998. xxi/887 pp. and xxiii/826 pp.

Every serious student of Ezekiel needs to own this commentary. Block writes very clearly and exposits this very difficult prophecy in an accessible manner. It is long, but he uses the pages to good purpose. He interacts with other commentaries without making it too tedious. MS★★★★★

Brownlee, W. H. *Ezekiel 1–19*. WBC. Nelson/Paternoster, 1986. xlii/320 pp.

Brownlee had a high view of Scripture, but this did not prevent him from seeing considerable editorial activity and redaction over a long period of time, resulting in the book that we have before us. Yet "despite all this editorial activity, the major contents of the book of Ezekiel are genuine, and whatever editing they later received serves to emphasize the prophet's greatness" (xl). MS★★★

Cooper, L. E., Sr. *Ezekiel*. NAC. Broadman, 1994. 440 pp.

This commentary is informative on a basic level but not too profound or thought-provoking. It adopts a dispensationalist and premillennial approach, which I personally find difficult to accept. So if that is your view, add a star. LM★★

Craigie, P. C. *Ezekiel*. DSB. Westminster John Knox, 1983. x/321 pp.

Craigie's brief yet helpful commentary is extremely readable. It opens up this difficult book for the interested lay reader. It takes an evangelical approach to the book. LM★★★★

Duguid, I. *Ezekiel*. NIVAC. Zondervan/Hodder & Stoughton, 1999. 568 pp.

Duguid's volume is an excellent example of the strengths of the NIVAC series. He is known in the scholarly world as a leading analyst of the prophet, but he has also served as a minister, and his pastoral sensitivities come through in this accessible commentary on an often-enigmatic prophet. LM★★★★★

Eichrodt, W. *Ezekiel*. OTL. Westminster John Knox/SCM, 1970. xiv/594 pp.

This volume is a translation of a work originally published in German in 1965/66. Eichrodt's moderately critical approach in the main agrees with the biblical presentation of Ezekiel and his ministry. Eichrodt applies a critical methodology that he believes does reveal some non-Ezekiel passages, but what is left, in his opinion, is without a doubt original. S★★★

Greenberg, M. *Ezekiel 1–20*. AYBC. Yale University Press, 1983.
Ezekiel 21–37. AYBC. Yale University Press, 1997. xv/388 pp.
and 371 pp.

This is a very interesting commentary on the book of Ezekiel.
Greenberg is well aware of what he is trying to accomplish as a
commentator (see *Ezekiel 1–20*, 18–27). He advocates what he calls
a holistic approach, which basically treats the MT as it stands and
as a whole. Very stimulating. MS★★★★

Hals, R. M. *Ezekiel*. FOTL. Eerdmans, 1989. xiii/363 pp.

Well researched and well written, but definitely, like the series as a
whole, geared to scholars. If ministers or students delve into this
book, the most helpful sections will be those concerning bibliography, structure, and intention. S★★★★

Jenson, R. W. *Ezekiel*. BTCB. Brazos, 2009. 367 pp.

A systematic theologian, Jenson offers a christological, Trinitarian,
ecclesial reading of the prophet from the perspective of the Nicene
Creed. He well recognizes the historical context of the prophet but
sometimes blurs the distinctive voice of the prophet in that setting
with a New Testament/theological reflection on his message. Still
very interesting and profitable though perhaps should be used in
tandem with a more historical-grammatical/critical commentary.
MS★★★★

Taylor, J. B. *Ezekiel*. TOTC. InterVarsity, 1969. 285 pp.

This commentary is especially designed for those who know little
about Ezekiel. It is conservative and easy to read. LM★★

Wevers, J. W. *Ezekiel*. NCB. Sheffield/Marshall Pickering, 1969.
x/355 pp.

Wevers presents a more traditional critical approach than Greenberg
and is a lot less stimulating than other critical scholars, especially
Zimmerli. S★★

Zimmerli, W. *Ezekiel*. 2 vols. Hermeneia. Fortress/SCM, 1979, 1982. xlvi/509 pp. and xxxiv/606 pp.

The German original was published in 1969. An English translation was long anticipated because of Zimmerli's breadth of knowledge and incredible insight. Zimmerli represents the best of critical thought on the book of Ezekiel. MS★★★↵

DANIEL

Baldwin, J. G. *Daniel*. TOTC. InterVarsity, 1978. 210 pp.

Although short, this commentary contains a wealth of information and careful exegetical insight. Baldwin is a balanced and sane exegete, which is important to note in a commentary on a book that attracts some wild ideas. Baldwin is solidly conservative but not rigid. LM★★★★

Collins, J. J. *Daniel*. FOTL. Eerdmans, 1984. xii/120 pp.

A very competent form-critical analysis and summary of discussion of Daniel. The book is technical and for that reason will only really interest scholars. S★★★★

Collins, J. J. *Daniel*. Hermeneia. Fortress/SCM, 1993. 498 pp.

The lengthy and extremely informative introduction includes an essay by A. Y. Collins, "The Influence of Daniel on the New Testament." J. J. Collins is a noted Daniel expert, and this volume is the apex of his decades-long research. It is critical in its approach, but evangelicals can learn much from this volume. MS★★★★★

Goldingay, J. *Daniel*. WBC. Nelson/Paternoster, 1989. liii/351 pp.

Goldingay's is perhaps the most comprehensive commentary on Daniel listed here. He gives insight into historical, literary, and theological issues concerning the book. He also demonstrates an amazing grasp of the secondary literature. Many of his readers will be put off by some of his radical (at least for an evangelical) conclusions, most notable of which are that the stories in chapters 1–6 are fictitious and the visions are quasi-prophecies. However, it would be a major mistake to ignore this important commentary while studying Daniel. MS★★★✔

Hartman, L. F., and A. A. Dilella. *The Book of Daniel*. AYBC. Yale University Press, 1978. xiv/345 pp.

This is one of the skimpier volumes in the Anchor Yale Bible Commentary series. It takes a typically critical approach to the date of the book. The exegetical comments are not that helpful. S★

Hill, A. E. *Daniel*. REBC 8. Zondervan, 2008. Pp. 19–212.

Hill writes with sensitivity to the theological message of the book. He supports the traditional view that the first-person apocalyptic vision reports of Daniel in chapters 7–12 go back to the sixth-century prophet. LM★★★★

Lacocque, A. *The Book of Daniel*. Westminster John Knox/SPCK, 1979. xxvi/302 pp.

This is an English translation of a French commentary originally published in 1976. Although he does provide some helpful textual and philological notes, Lacocque is strong on theology and contemporary application (at least relatively so for a critical scholar). He adopts a traditional critical dating and interpretation. MS★★★

Longman, T., III. *Daniel*. NIVAC. Zondervan/Hodder & Stoughton, 1999. 313 pp.

In keeping with the design of the NIVAC series, I explore the original meaning and contemporary significance of this interesting, yet often-enigmatic, biblical book. In addition, I explain how I move from the ancient text to our modern situation. Daniel becomes, in the first six chapters, a study of how a person of faith not only copes but even thrives in a hostile cultural setting. In the last half of the book, it raises the question of how we are to understand the apocalyptic sections of Scripture that describe the end of history. The theme of the whole book is that in spite of present difficult circumstances, God is in control and will defeat the forces of evil and oppression. LM

Lucas, E. C. *Daniel*. AOTC. InterVarsity, 2002. 359 pp.

Lucas is sensitive to Daniel as literature and theology. He provides a special study of the ancient Near Eastern background to the imagery in chapters 7–12. Many, however, including myself, will find his arguments in favor of a second-century date for the book weak, though he does argue in a way that is consistent with a high view of biblical authority. MS★★★

Miller, S. M. *Daniel*. NAC. Broadman, 1994. 348 pp.

Miller writes competently in defense of a conservative approach to the book. He concentrates on historical issues and the basic theological message. In the apocalyptic sections, he adopts a literal (plain) reading of the text. LM★★★

Porteous, N. W. *Daniel*. OTL. Westminster John Knox/SCM, 1965. 173 pp.

Porteous concentrates on theology, not language. The commentary is short. Porteous adopts a critical stance toward the book. S★★

Redditt, P. L. *Daniel*. NCB. Sheffield Academic Press, 1999. 211 pp.

Redditt gives a rather uninspired traditional critical reading to the book of Daniel. MS⇥

Russell, D. S. *Daniel*. DSB. Westminster John Knox, 1981. 244 pp.

Russell is one of the previous generation's leading critical interpreters of apocalyptic literature. In his introduction, he dates the book late and gives a very unsatisfactory explanation of pseudonymity. However, his insistence on the present relevance of the book (over against a speculative futuristic approach) has much to commend itself. LM★★★

Towner, W. S. *Daniel*. Interp. Westminster John Knox, 1984. xi/186 pp.

This commentary concentrates on the theology of the book and is written from a critical perspective. The writing is clear and often insightful. MS★★★

Wallace, R. S. *The Lord Is King: The Message of Daniel*. BST. InterVarsity, 1979. 200 pp.

Wallace has written a good, popular exposition from an evangelical perspective. Solid research backs up his comments. The introduction provides a helpful conservative defense against a late dating of the book. LM★★★★

Young, E. J. *The Prophecy of Daniel*. Banner of Truth, 1949. 330 pp.

The importance of this commentary is found in its firm and intelligent conservative stance. Young polemicizes against critical and dispensationalist approaches. He is not particularly sensitive to the literary nature or biblical theology of the book, but he is an excellent language scholar. MS★★★

HOSEA

Achtemeier, E. *Minor Prophets I*. UBCS. Baker Books, 1996. 390 pp.

Achtemeier produces a good, solid, but not particularly exciting exegesis of the Minor Prophets through Micah. LM★★★

Andersen, F. I., and D. N. Freedman. *Hosea*. AYBC. Yale University Press, 1980. xvii/701 pp.

This massive commentary is one of the best on any biblical book. For one thing, the authors are permitted the space to do a fuller job of commenting on the Hebrew text. Both authors are well-known, respected linguists. Andersen has some theological sense. The book is marred a little by a syllable-counting approach to meter. MS★★★★

Carroll R. (Rodas), M. Daniel. *Hosea*. REBC 8. Zondervan, 2008. Pp. 213–305.

Carroll packs a lot of content and substance into his commentary on Hosea. It is a clear and profound look at the theology of the prophet in his historical context. LM★★★★½

Craigie, P. C. *Twelve Prophets*. 2 vols. DSB. Westminster John Knox, 1985. ix/239 pp. and 272 pp.

As in most series, the Minor Prophets get short shrift in terms of space. This does not mean that the present commentary is worthless; Craigie is too insightful for that. It is only that it could be so much better if twice as many pages were allocated to the Minor Prophets. LM★★★

Dearman, J. A. *The Book of Hosea*. NICOT. Eerdmans, 2010. xiv/408 pp.

Hosea is a complex book, but Dearman is up to the task. As a Hebraist, he provides an excellent translation of the difficult Hebrew. His literary and historical skills help him unravel difficult exegetical issues. He is also sensitive to Hosea's theological contribution. MS★★★★★

Garrett, D. A. *Hosea, Joel*. NAC. Broadman, 1997. 426 pp.

See under Joel.

Hubbard, D. A. *Hosea*. TOTC. InterVarsity, 1989. 234 pp.

Hubbard's commentary on Hosea is proportionately one of the most extensive in the series. His commentary on the fourteen chapters of Hosea is nearly as long as Baldwin's on 1 and 2 Samuel. Hubbard takes full advantage of this fact to provide a compellingly written, thoughtful analysis of Hosea's prophecy. Hosea is one of the more difficult books of the Bible to interpret. His commentary is based on sound scholarship and extensive research and is extremely readable. LM★★★★

Kidner, D. *The Message of Hosea: Love to the Loveless*. BST. Inter-Varsity, 1981. 142 pp.

This volume is one of the most engaging in the series. Kidner, with his usual skill, combines scholarship, pastoral insight, and concern with a vital writing style. LM★★✔

Limburg, J. *Hosea–Micah*. Interp. Westminster John Knox, 1988. xi/201 pp.

This readable commentary concentrates on themes in selected texts. Brief, but very stimulating. LM★★★

Mays, J. L. *Hosea*. OTL. Westminster John Knox/SCM, 1969. x/190 pp.

Mays concentrates on the theological meaning of the text to the subordination of philology, text, and other exegetical concerns. He comes from a moderately critical perspective. MS★★★

McComiskey, T. "Hosea." In *The Minor Prophets: An Exegetical and Expository Commentary*. Ed. T. McComiskey. Vol. 1. Baker, 1992. Pp. 1–237.

For serious study of Hosea, this commentary is a must. The volume offers both close reading of the Hebrew and a separate exposition of the book. An important commentary for those who preach on the book. Also included in this volume are commentaries on Joel

by R. B. Dillard and J. Niehaus on Amos (see under those books).
MS★★★★★

Smith, G. V. *Hosea/Amos/Micah.* NIVAC. Zondervan/Hodder &
Stoughton, 2001. 596 pp.

See under Amos.

Stuart, D. *Hosea–Jonah.* WBC. Nelson/Paternoster, 1987.
xlv/537 pp.

This is one of the best recent commentaries on the Minor Prophets.
It is a must-buy for everyone preaching on these books. It is intel-
ligently conservative and emphasizes theology without ignoring
the other aspects of the text. Shows how these prophets operated
in a tradition going back to the covenant curses of the Pentateuch.
MS★★★★

Vawter, B. *Amos, Hosea, Micah, with an Introduction to Classical
Poetry.* OTM. Michael Glazier, 1981. 169 pp.

See under Amos.

Wolff, H. W. *Hosea.* Hermeneia. Fortress/SCM, 1974.
xxiii/259 pp.

Originally published in German in 1965, Wolff's work on Hosea
has been the most influential force in Hosea studies for more than
two decades. This is an excellent commentary on all aspects of the
text and is written from a critical perspective. S★★★★

JOEL

Achtemeier, E. *Minor Prophets I.* UBCS. Baker Books, 1996.
390 pp.

See under Hosea.

Allen, L. C. *Joel, Obadiah, Jonah, and Micah*. NICOT. Eerdmans, 1976. 427 pp.

See under Jonah.

Baker, D. W. *Joel, Obadiah, Malachi*. NIVAC. Zondervan/Hodder & Stoughton, 2006. 341 pp.

Baker writes clearly as he skillfully exposits the meaning and application of these three Minor Prophets. He writes not only as a skilled Old Testament scholar but also as someone very in touch with life. LM★★★★

Barton, J. *Joel and Obadiah*. OTL. Westminster John Knox/SCM, 2001. xxi/168 pp.

See also under Obadiah. He dates Joel to the early Second Temple, but the second half of Joel may be later. MS★★★★

Coggins, R. J. *Joel and Amos*. NCB. Sheffield Academic Press, 2000. 168 pp.

See under Amos.

Craigie, P. C. *Twelve Prophets*. 2 vols. DSB. Westminster John Knox, 1985. ix/239 pp. and 272 pp.

See under Hosea.

Crenshaw, J. L. *Joel*. AYBC. Yale University Press, 1995. 240 pp.

Crenshaw delivers an incisive commentary on the book, examining the literary nature as well as historical background and theological message. He questions whether Joel attributes the suffering of God's people to their sin, since the text nowhere makes this connection. However, the answer to the suffering is clear: Yahweh. MS★★✔

Dillard, R. B. "Joel." In *The Minor Prophets: An Exegetical and Expository Commentary*. Ed. T. McComiskey. Vol. 1. Baker, 1992. Pp. 239–313.

Dillard has written a thoughtful and profound commentary on this intriguing biblical book. It combines an excellent technical investigation (philology, text, etc.) with an interesting theological study. If you get only one commentary on Joel, this should be it. MS★★★★★

Finley, T. J. *Joel, Amos, Obadiah*. WEC. Moody, 1990. 417 pp.

This is a fully conceived commentary interested in all aspects of the biblical books that it studies. There are comments about history, literary matters, theology, philology, and practical application. Finley takes careful and reasoned positions. His writing style is clear and interesting. MS★★★★

Garrett, D. A. *Hosea, Joel*. NAC. Broadman, 1997. 426 pp.

Garrett is a clear writer who reaches his exegetical conclusions in a reasoned manner and with appropriate restraint, qualities needed in the treatment of these two books whose study entails contact with many controversies. LM★★★★

Hubbard, D. A. *Joel and Amos*. TOTC. InterVarsity, 1989. 245 pp.

This volume is brief, yet well written and very useful—particularly in the areas of historical background, theology, and application. LM★★★★

Limburg, J. *Hosea–Micah*. Interp. Westminster John Knox, 1988. xi/201 pp.

See under Hosea.

Patterson, R. D. *Joel*. REBC 8. Zondervan, 2008. Pp. 307–46.

Patterson is a careful exegete who is sensitive to the literary quality of the book. He tentatively dates Joel to the second half of the eighth century BC. The prophet uses a historical locust plague to warn Judah to repent before a more serious judgment comes on them. LM★★★✓

Stuart, D. *Hosea–Jonah*. WBC. Nelson/Paternoster, 1987. xlv/537 pp.

See under Hosea.

Watts, J. D. W. *The Books of Joel, Obadiah, Jonah, Nahum, Habakkuk, and Zephaniah*. CBC. Cambridge University Press, 1975. x/190 pp.

There are short, helpful introductions to each book. Watts explores the connection between these books and the day of the Lord and worship themes. He argues that these prophecies are prophetic liturgies. LM★★★

Wolff, H. W. *Joel and Amos*. Hermeneia. Fortress/SCM, 1977. xxiv/392 pp.

This commentary was written originally in German in 1969 and is a benchmark study of both books. Written from a moderately critical perspective. MS★★★★

AMOS

Achtemeier, E. *Minor Prophets I*. UBCS. Baker Books, 1996. 390 pp.

See under Hosea.

Andersen, F. I., and D. N. Freedman. *Amos*. AYBC. Yale University Press, 1989. xliii/977 pp.

This massive commentary is obviously not for those who are only casually interested in the book of Amos. The incredible detail is especially welcomed by the scholar as well as the seminary student and studious pastor. The authors are explicit about their method, and much can be carried over to the study of other biblical books. The commentary focuses on the final form of the text. It explains the changes in Amos's message by "dynamic developments in the prophet's career" rather than by a later editor who radically transforms his message. They do see evidence of editorial activity, but observe a "coherence between prophet and editor" (74). There is a lot of information in this commentary. It is a must for those who really want to delve into the Hebrew text of Amos. MS★★★✦

Coggins, R. J. *Joel and Amos*. NCB. Sheffield Academic Press, 2000. 168 pp.

A rather unremarkable commentary taking a traditional critical line on the books. MS★★

Craigie, P. C. *Twelve Prophets*. 2 vols. DSB. Westminster John Knox, 1985. ix/239 pp. and 272 pp.

See under Hosea.

Hubbard, D. A. *Joel and Amos*. TOTC. InterVarsity, 1989. 245 pp.

See under Joel.

Jeremias, J. *The Book of Amos*. OTL. Westminster John Knox/ SCM, 1998. 200 pp.

Jeremias reads Amos as predominantly written after the vision of the future it purports to describe, that is, after the fall of the north and even some parts as late as the fall of the south. He concerns himself largely with delineating and describing hypothetical editions of the book. S★★★

Limburg, J. *Hosea–Micah*. Interp. Westminster John Knox, 1988. xi/201 pp.

See under Hosea.

Mays, J. L. *Amos*. OTL. Westminster John Knox/SCM, 1969. 176 pp.

Mays provides an extensive treatment of the book from a moderately critical perspective. He presents philological and other technical analyses but does not lose sight of the theological message of the book. MS★★★★

McComiskey, T. E., and T. Longman III. *Amos*. REBC 8. Zondervan, 2008. Pp. 347–420.

Truth be told, my role was simply to update the deceased McComiskey's earlier commentary. As I worked on this commentary, I came to appreciate McComiskey's careful exegesis, though it is not quite as strong in biblical theology. LM★★★✦

Motyer, J. A. *Amos: The Day of the Lion*. BST. InterVarsity, 1974. 208 pp.

This volume, one of the first in the series, is well written by a competent and popular expositor. Although popular, the volume does have substantial research behind it. LM★★★

Niehaus, J. "Amos." In *The Minor Prophets: An Exegetical and Expository Commentary*. Ed. T. McComiskey. Vol. 1. Baker, 1992. Pp. 315–494.

The strength of this commentary is in its sensitivity to historical background and reference. This approach is aided by the author's competence in archaeology and ancient Near Eastern studies. The concept of covenant is fully exposed in relationship to this eighth-century prophet. MS★★★★

Paul, S. M. *Amos.* Hermeneia. Fortress/SCM, 1991. xxvii/406 pp.

This is the second Amos commentary in the series (see Wolff). Paul's commentary is to be preferred for its interest in the text's integrity. As opposed to Wolff, who posits six redactional layers to the book, Paul ascribes virtually the whole book to Amos. He writes clearly, and his work is extremely well researched. MS★★★★★

Smith, B. K., and F. S. Page. *Amos, Obadiah, Jonah.* NAC. Broadman, 1995. 304 pp.

See also under Obadiah and Jonah. Smith wrote the commentary on Amos. It is a competent commentary with a clear introduction to the historical background of the book. LM★★★

Smith, G. V. *Amos: A Commentary.* 2nd ed. Mentor Commentaries. Christian Focus, 1998. 398 pp.

Smith has produced a magisterial treatment of the book of Amos from an evangelical perspective. He exegetes the text with extensive treatment of text, philology, literary structure, and theological message. MS★★★★

Smith, G. V. *Hosea/Amos/Micah.* NIVAC. Zondervan/Hodder & Stoughton, 2001. 596 pp.

Smith has already written one of the most extensive scholarly treatments of the original meaning of the book of Amos. It is in the area of original meaning of all three of these early prophets that he is strongest. The sections on contemporary significance are often helpful but not quite as strong as in some of the other volumes of this series. LM★★★

Stuart, D. *Hosea–Jonah.* WBC. Nelson/Paternoster, 1987. xlv/537 pp.

See under Hosea.

Vawter, B. *Amos, Hosea, Micah, with an Introduction to Classical Poetry*. OTM. Michael Glazier, 1981. 169 pp.

This volume is a well-written and lucid presentation of three of the most prominent Minor Prophets and of prophecy in general. Written from a critical perspective. LM★★★

Wolff, H. W. *Joel and Amos*. Hermeneia. Fortress/SCM, 1977. xxiv/392 pp.

See under Joel.

OBADIAH

Achtemeier, E. *Minor Prophets I*. UBCS. Baker Books, 1996. 390 pp.

See under Hosea.

Allen, L. C. *Joel, Obadiah, Jonah, and Micah*. NICOT. Eerdmans, 1976. 427 pp.

See under Jonah.

Armerding, C. E. *Obadiah*. REBC 8. Zondervan, 2008. Pp. 421–49.

Clear and helpful. He places Obadiah post-586 BC and responding to the Edomite harassment of Judah after the destruction of Jerusalem. LM★★★★

Baker, D. W. *Joel, Obadiah, Malachi*. NIVAC. Zondervan/Hodder & Stoughton, 2006. 341 pp.

See under Joel.

Baker, D. W., T. D. Alexander, and B. K. Waltke. *Obadiah, Jonah, Micah*. TOTC. InterVarsity, 1988. 207 pp.

See also under Jonah and Micah. Baker wrote the section on Obadiah. He takes a highly competent, evangelical approach to the book, emphasizing historical background and theology. LM★★★★

Barton, J. *Joel and Obadiah*. OTL. Westminster John Knox/SCM, 2001. xxi/168 pp.

See also under Joel. A very well-executed historical-critical commentary on these two Minor Prophets. Barton refuses to focus on the final form and wants to find the original setting, which will make this commentary less interesting to most, though he is an engaging writer. Dates the first part of Obadiah to the exile, but states that the second half is an eschatological addition. MS★★★★

Craigie, P. C. *Twelve Prophets*. 2 vols. DSB. Westminster John Knox, 1985. ix/239 pp. and 272 pp.

See under Hosea.

Limburg, J. *Hosea–Micah*. Interp. Westminster John Knox, 1988. xi/201 pp.

See under Hosea.

Niehaus, J. "Obadiah." In *The Minor Prophets: An Exegetical and Expository Commentary*. Ed. T. McComiskey. Vol. 2. Baker, 1993. Pp. 495–541.

Niehaus gives us one of the most extensive treatments of this short book. He combines historical, literary, and theological insight in this helpful commentary. He is open to the position that the author is the same person who plays an important role in the Elijah-Ahab narrative (1 Kings 18:1). LM★★★★

Raabe, P. R. *Obadiah*. AYBC. Yale University Press, 1996.
xxvi/310 pp.

This is an excellent commentary on the smallest book of the Old
Testament. It is very thorough in discussion of words, historical
issues, literary forms, and controversies. It deals with the meaning
of the text but not too extensively with its canonical significance.
MS★★★★★

Smith, B. K., and F. S. Page. *Amos, Obadiah, Jonah*. NAC. Broadman, 1995. 304 pp.

Smith's Obadiah commentary is not quite as strong as his contribution on Amos (see above). Lacks detail and interest. LM★★★

Stuart, D. *Hosea–Jonah*. WBC. Nelson/Paternoster, 1987.
xlv/537 pp.

See under Hosea.

Watts, J. D. W. *The Books of Joel, Obadiah, Jonah, Nahum, Habakkuk, and Zephaniah*. CBC. Cambridge University Press,
1975. x/190 pp.

See under Joel.

Wolff, H. W. *Obadiah and Jonah*. CC. Fortress, 1986. 191 pp.

See under Jonah.

JONAH

Achtemeier, E. *Minor Prophets I*. UBCS. Baker Books, 1996.
390 pp.

See under Hosea.

Allen, L. C. *Joel, Obadiah, Jonah, and Micah.* NICOT. Eerdmans, 1976. 427 pp.

Allen provides an up-to-date, insightful, and careful commentary on these interesting books. He writes with literary sensitivity, although many evangelicals will disagree with some of his conclusions. MS★★★

Baker, D. W., T. D. Alexander, and B. K. Waltke. *Obadiah, Jonah, Micah.* TOTC. InterVarsity, 1988. 207 pp.

See also under Obadiah and Micah. T. D. Alexander wrote the section on Jonah. Like the other authors in the book, Alexander provides a very helpful guide to the historical background and theology of the book. Alexander also provides a very interesting discussion of the genre of the book and concludes that it is didactic history writing. LM★★★★

Baldwin, J. G. "Jonah." In *The Minor Prophets: An Exegetical and Expository Commentary.* Ed. T. McComiskey. Vol. 2. Baker, 1993. Pp. 543–90.

Baldwin is always highly worth reading on any book on which she chooses to comment. In the case of Jonah, she is equaled by some others, but this is worthwhile. MS★★★

Bruckner, J. *Jonah, Nahum, Habakkuk, Zephaniah.* NIVAC. Zondervan/Hodder & Stoughton, 2004. 356 pp.

Bruckner does a nice job getting to the heart of the message of the book and provides excellent discussions of the continuing relevance of these four prophetic messages in terms both of their theology and of their practical significance. I found the discussion of Jonah the most stimulating, though the others are good as well. LM★★★

Cary, P. *Jonah.* BTCB. Brazos, 2008. 187 pp.

As is the case in this series, Cary provides a Christian reading of the book of Jonah, avoiding a moralistic approach which he takes as anti-Semitic. While I am not convinced that a moralistic approach has to be anti-Semitic, I applaud his christological approach. MS★★★✔

Craigie, P. C. *Twelve Prophets*. 2 vols. DSB. Westminster John Knox, 1985. ix/239 pp. and 272 pp.

See under Hosea.

Limburg, J. *Jonah*. OTL. Westminster John Knox/SCM, 1993. 144 pp.

This book is a fine summary statement of a moderate critical analysis of the literary and theological dimensions of the book of Jonah. It is well written with interesting comments about the use of the book in the New Testament, later Judaism, and Islam, as well as on music and art. MS★★★★

Sasson, J. M. *Jonah*. AYBC. Yale University Press, 1990. xvi/368 pp.

This provocative commentary on the literary gem Jonah is well worth adding to a reference library. It not only rehearses previous views but suggestively presents its own reading of the book. MS★★★★★

Simon, U. *Jonah*. JPS Bible Commentary. Jewish Publication Society, 1999. xliii/52 pp.

On the basis of its "nonrealistic mode of composition," Simon defines the genre of Jonah as "theological prophetic history." He believes that the book's theme is the contest between justice and compassion. The character Jonah takes the side of a strict justice, to which God (and the book) objects. LM★✔

Smith, B. K., and F. S. Page. *Amos, Obadiah, Jonah*. NAC. Broadman, 1995. 304 pp.

See also under Amos and Obadiah. Page wrote the Jonah commentary. The introduction, among other things, presents a strong, well-argued case for taking the book of Jonah as a historical, not fictional, work. Page also brings forward the best insights into the literary quality of the book. LM★★★

Stuart, D. *Hosea–Jonah*. WBC. Nelson/Paternoster, 1987. xlv/537 pp.

See under Hosea.

Walton, J. H. *Jonah*. REBC 8. Zondervan, 2008. Pp. 451–99.

Walton has a wonderful knowledge of ancient Near Eastern background and great exegetical sensitivity. He often has interesting takes on biblical books and is always worth consulting. This commentary is no exception. He understands the book's main purpose as teaching that the prophets' prophetic pronouncements are by no means irreversible and may be forestalled or avoided by repentance that elicits God's compassion. LM★★★★★

Watts, J. D. W. *The Books of Joel, Obadiah, Jonah, Nahum, Habakkuk, and Zephaniah*. CBC. Cambridge University Press, 1975. x/190 pp.

See under Joel.

Wolff, H. W. *Obadiah and Jonah*. CC. Fortress, 1986. 191 pp.

Wolff combines excellent philological ability with theological insight to produce a very helpful commentary on these two prophetic books. His stance is moderately critical. The format of the commentary makes his comments easy to get at. Good textual criticism. MS★★★★

MICAH

Achtemeier, E. *Minor Prophets I*. UBCS. Baker Books, 1996. 390 pp.

See under Hosea.

Allen, L. C. *Joel, Obadiah, Jonah, and Micah.* NICOT. Eerdmans, 1976. 427 pp.

See under Jonah.

Andersen, F. I., and D. N. Freedman. *Micah.* AYBC. Yale University Press, 2000. 637 pp.

As one can tell from the length, this is the fullest treatment of the book of Micah in recent times. The authors, both senior members of the guild of Old Testament studies, have thoroughly researched the book and also canvassed the secondary literature. The exegetical conclusions are not always satisfying, and the authors have little interest in broader theological issues, but for what it is, it is excellent. MS★★★★

Baker, D. W., T. D. Alexander, and B. K. Waltke. *Obadiah, Jonah, Micah.* TOTC. InterVarsity, 1988. 207 pp.

See also under Obadiah and Jonah. Waltke wrote the section on Micah. It is the distillation of careful scholarship presented in an engaging format for the lay reader. LM★★★★★

Barker, K. L., and W. Bailey. *Micah, Nahum, Habakkuk, Zephaniah.* NAC. Broadman, 1999. 528 pp.

See also under Nahum and Zephaniah. Barker's Micah commentary is a good, competent commentary written from a premillennial perspective. However, the depth of research as indicated by the footnotes looks a bit dated. LM★★★

ben Zvi, Ehud. *Micah.* FOTL. Eerdmans, 2000. xvi/189 pp.

Ben Zvi has produced the most comprehensive analysis of the form-critical nature of the prophet. He has some very interesting comments on the fact that Micah is a book that is constantly reread. Even those who will not accept the conclusions of his analysis—and many evangelicals will not—will still find this commentary a useful compendium of other people's opinions. S★★★★

Craigie, P. C. *Twelve Prophets*. 2 vols. DSB. Westminster John Knox, 1985. ix/239 pp. and 272 pp.

See under Hosea.

Hillers, D. R. *Micah*. Hermeneia. Fortress/SCM, 1984. xviii/192 pp.

Hillers avoids redaction criticism as too speculative. He approaches the book as a whole rather than diachronically. He sees Micah's oracles as a part of a "revitalization" program, which protests oppression and looks to a new age. This commentary should be consulted by serious students. MS★★★

Limburg, J. *Hosea–Micah*. Interp. Westminster John Knox, 1988. xi/201 pp.

See under Hosea.

Mays, J. L. *Micah*. OTL. Westminster John Knox/SCM, 1976. xii/169 pp.

A rare one-volume commentary on Micah. This is a well-written commentary that deserves close attention. Mays is a good scholar in the critical school. He communicates well and provides a well-rounded commentary. MS★★★

McComiskey, T. E., and T. Longman III. *Micah*. REBC 8. Zondervan, 2008. Pp. 491–551.

As with McComiskey's Amos commentary, my role was to bring his commentary up-to-date in the revision that took place after his death. This short commentary is a good orientation to the interpretation of the book, but for more see the lengthier work by Waltke. LM★★★↲

Smith, G. V. *Hosea/Amos/Micah*. NIVAC. Zondervan/Hodder & Stoughton, 2001. 596 pp.

See under Amos.

Smith, R. L. *Micah–Malachi*. WBC. Nelson/Paternoster, 1984. xvii/358 pp.

This commentary is solid and competent. It is hampered by size restrictions. The section on Nahum, for example, is extremely scanty and not particularly original. LM★★

Vawter, B. *Amos, Hosea, Micah, with an Introduction to Classical Poetry*. OTM. Michael Glazier, 1981. 169 pp.

See under Amos.

Waltke, B. K. *A Commentary on Micah*. Eerdmans, 2007. xviii/490 pp.

Waltke has written the most comprehensive and insightful commentary on the book of Micah available today. He addresses both interpretation and application. He discusses all the important interpretive debates and has mastered the secondary literature. While the amount of information and the detail of his interpretation appeals mainly to professionals, the motivated layperson will also find this helpful. For a shorter version of his interpretive approach to the book, see his contribution to the McComiskey edited series listed below. LM★★★★★

Waltke, B. K. "Micah." In *The Minor Prophets: An Exegetical and Expository Commentary*. Ed. T. McComiskey. Vol. 2. Baker, 1993. Pp. 591–764.

This is a fuller form of Waltke's TOTC commentary and is the best volume on the book. The author comments on all aspects of the book. LM★★★★★

NAHUM

Achtemeier, E. *Nahum–Malachi*. Interp. Westminster John Knox, 1986. x/201 pp.

An insightful commentary from a moderately critical perspective. LM★★★

Armerding, C. E. *Nahum*. REBC 8. Zondervan, 2008. Pp. 535–601.

Helpful, brief, and clear. Very informative. LM★★★↗

Baker, D. W. *Nahum, Habakkuk, and Zephaniah*. TOTC. Inter-Varsity, 1988. 121 pp.

Baker's commentary shares the strengths of the series: an engaging writing style and an emphasis on theology and historical background. LM★★★★

Barker, K. L., and W. Bailey. *Micah, Nahum, Habakkuk, Zephaniah*. NAC. Broadman, 1999. 528 pp.

See also under Micah and Zephaniah. Bailey has contributed a strongly written, well-thought-out, and well-researched analysis of Nahum that is sensitive to the important theological themes. LM★★★★

Boadt, L. *Jeremiah 26–52, Habakkuk, Zephaniah, Nahum*. OTM. Michael Glazier, 1982. xii/276 pp.

See under Jeremiah.

Bruckner, J. *Jonah, Nahum, Habakkuk, Zephaniah*. NIVAC. Zondervan/Hodder & Stoughton, 2004. 356 pp.

See under Jonah.

Craigie, P. C. *Twelve Prophets*. 2 vols. DSB. Westminster John Knox, 1985. ix/239 pp. and 272 pp.

See under Hosea.

Floyd, M. H. *Minor Prophets, Part 2*. FOTL. Eerdmans, 2000. xviii/641 pp.

An excellent form-critical study of these prophets, not only of the whole books but of their parts. Floyd does a better job than most connecting this narrow topic with the broader issues of interpretation. Nonetheless, this excellent work will only be helpful to scholars. S★★★★★

Longman, T., III. "Nahum." In *The Minor Prophets: An Exegetical and Expository Commentary*. Ed. T. McComiskey. Vol. 2. Baker, 1993. Pp. 765–829.

This volume shows the relevance of the book for today by explicating the theme of God as a warrior. MS

Patterson, R. D. *Nahum, Habakkuk, Zephaniah*. WEC. Moody, 1991. xxv/416 pp.

See also under Habakkuk and Zephaniah. Patterson shows tremendous literary sensitivity to Nahum. He also places the book in its historical context. He falls short in the theology of the book by emphasizing God's sovereignty but not adequately discussing the divine warrior theme. MS★★★★

Roberts, J. J. M. *Nahum, Habakkuk, and Zephaniah*. OTL. Westminster John Knox/SCM, 1991. 223 pp.

This commentary is another helpful addition to the study of these three Minor Prophets. There are extensive text-critical and philological notes, written in a way that even interested nonspecialists can understand. Roberts is more optimistic than most these days about the benefits of historical criticism. MS★★★★

Robertson, O. P. *The Books of Nahum, Habakkuk, and Zephaniah*. NICOT. Eerdmans, 1990. x/357 pp.

This commentary gives significant attention to three of the more interesting, but often-neglected, Minor Prophets. Robertson excels in theological analysis and pastoral application. The commentary is weak in philological and other technical studies. LM★★◂

Smith, R. L. *Micah–Malachi.* WBC. Nelson/Paternoster, 1984. xvii/358 pp.

See under Micah.

Watts, J. D. W. *The Books of Joel, Obadiah, Jonah, Nahum, Habakkuk, and Zephaniah.* CBC. Cambridge University Press, 1975. x/190 pp.

See under Joel.

HABAKKUK

Achtemeier, E. *Nahum–Malachi.* Interp. Westminster John Knox, 1986. x/201 pp.

See under Nahum.

Andersen, F. I. *Habakkuk.* AYBC. Yale University Press, 2001. xxii/387 pp.

Andersen has produced an excellent scholarly reading of the prophet Habakkuk. In his preface he expresses the desire to communicate with the nontechnical reader, and he indeed is a very clear writer. However, the depth of his analysis and the choice of his topics make this commentary better suited for the scholar and occasional minister. MS★★★★

Armerding, C. E. *Habakkuk.* REBC 8. Zondervan, 2008. Pp. 603–48.

Helpful, brief, and clear. Very informative. LM★★★◂

Baker, D. W. *Nahum, Habakkuk, and Zephaniah.* TOTC. Inter-Varsity, 1988. 121 pp.

See under Nahum.

Barker, K. L., and W. Bailey. *Micah, Nahum, Habakkuk, Zephaniah*. NAC. Broadman, 1999. 528 pp.

See under Zephaniah.

Boadt, L. *Jeremiah 26–52, Habakkuk, Zephaniah, Nahum*. OTM. Michael Glazier, 1982. xii/276 pp.

See under Jeremiah.

Bruce, F. F. "Habakkuk." In *The Minor Prophets: An Exegetical and Expository Commentary*. Ed. T. McComiskey. Vol. 2. Baker, 1993. Pp. 831–96.

Normally identified as a New Testament scholar, the erudite Bruce is also highly competent on this Old Testament subject. MS★★★

Bruckner, J. *Jonah, Nahum, Habakkuk, Zephaniah*. NIVAC. Zondervan/Hodder & Stoughton, 2004. 356 pp.

See under Jonah.

Craigie, P. C. *Twelve Prophets*. 2 vols. DSB. Westminster John Knox, 1985. ix/239 pp. and 272 pp.

See under Hosea.

Floyd, M. H. *Minor Prophets, Part 2*. FOTL. Eerdmans, 2000. xviii/641 pp.

See under Nahum.

Patterson, R. D. *Nahum, Habakkuk, Zephaniah*. WEC. Moody, 1991. xxv/416 pp.

See also under Nahum and Zephaniah. This commentary may be the best, in terms of quantity as well as quality of insight, on this Minor Prophet. It is particularly strong on literary and historical analysis. It is also helpful in its comments on theology but would have benefited from a stronger sense of the divine warrior theme. MS★★★★

Roberts, J. J. M. *Nahum, Habakkuk, and Zephaniah*. OTL. West-minster John Knox/SCM, 1991. 223 pp.

See under Nahum.

Robertson, O. P. *The Books of Nahum, Habakkuk, and Zepha-niah*. NICOT. Eerdmans, 1990. x/357 pp.

See under Nahum.

Smith, R. L. *Micah–Malachi*. WBC Nelson/Paternoster, 1984. xvii/358 pp.

See under Micah.

Watts, J. D. W. *The Books of Joel, Obadiah, Jonah, Nahum, Ha-bakkuk, and Zephaniah*. CBC. Cambridge University Press, 1975. x/190 pp.

See under Joel.

ZEPHANIAH

Achtemeier, E. *Nahum–Malachi*. Interp. Westminster John Knox, 1986. x/201 pp.

See under Nahum.

Baker, D. W. *Nahum, Habakkuk, and Zephaniah*. TOTC. Inter-Varsity, 1988. 121 pp.

See under Nahum.

Barker, K. L., and W. Bailey. *Micah, Nahum, Habakkuk, Zepha-niah*. NAC. Broadman, 1999. 528 pp.

See also under Micah and Nahum. Bailey's Zephaniah section is a good solid commentary. The introduction tends to spend a lot of time describing (rather than substantially critiquing) other viewpoints on controversial issues, but the reader still gets Bailey's own views. LM★★★

Berlin, A. *Zephaniah*. AYBC. Yale University Press, 1994. xvi/165 pp.

Berlin is known as an exceptional practitioner of the literary method, and she does not disappoint us in this commentary, which shows great sensitivity to such issues as intertextuality. She also helpfully discusses text, semantics, historical issues, and theological message. MS★★★★★

Boadt, L. *Jeremiah 26–52, Habakkuk, Zephaniah, Nahum*. OTM. Michael Glazier, 1982. xii/276 pp.

See under Jeremiah.

Bruckner, J. *Jonah, Nahum, Habakkuk, Zephaniah*. NIVAC. Zondervan/Hodder & Stoughton, 2004. 356 pp.

See under Jonah.

Craigie, P. C. *Twelve Prophets*. 2 vols. DSB. Westminster John Knox, 1985. ix/239 pp. and 272 pp.

See under Hosea.

Floyd, M. H. *Minor Prophets, Part 2*. FOTL. Eerdmans, 2000. xviii/641 pp.

See under Nahum.

Motyer, J. A. "Zephaniah." In *The Minor Prophets: An Exegetical and Expository Commentary*. Ed. T. McComiskey. Vol. 3. Baker, 1998. Pp. 897–962.

Motyer presents a readable and solid interpretation of Zephaniah. One of the more in-depth analyses. LM★★★★

Patterson, R. D. *Nahum, Habakkuk, Zephaniah*. WEC. Moody, 1991. xxv/416 pp.

As in his work on Nahum and Habakkuk (see above), Patterson does an excellent job on most aspects of the book. He is clear, engaging, and profound, particularly in areas of historical background and literary strategy. He does a good job on the theological message of the book, but improvement could be made here. MS★★★★

Roberts, J. J. M. *Nahum, Habakkuk, and Zephaniah*. OTL. Westminster John Knox/SCM, 1991. 223 pp.

See under Nahum.

Robertson, O. P. *The Books of Nahum, Habakkuk, and Zephaniah*. NICOT. Eerdmans, 1990. x/357 pp.

See under Nahum.

Smith, R. L. *Micah–Malachi*. WBC. Nelson/Paternoster, 1984. xvii/358 pp.

See under Micah.

Walker, L. L. *Zephaniah*. REBC 8. Zondervan, 2008. Pp. 649–95.

Notable in this concise but helpful commentary is attention to intertextuality. Good treatment of the theology of the book. LM★★★⁴

Watts, J. D. W. *The Books of Joel, Obadiah, Jonah, Nahum, Habakkuk, and Zephaniah*. CBC. Cambridge University Press, 1975. x/190 pp.

See under Joel.

HAGGAI

Achtemeier, E. *Nahum–Malachi*. Interp. Westminster John Knox, 1986. x/201 pp.

See under Nahum.

Baldwin, J. G. *Haggai, Zechariah, Malachi*. TOTC. InterVarsity, 1972. 253 pp.

A very insightful, conservative commentary. LM★★★

Boda, M. J. *Haggai, Zechariah*. NIVAC. Zondervan/Hodder & Stoughton, 2004. 576 pp.

This is one of the meatier commentaries in the NIVAC series. It provides a substantial discussion of introductory issues and the original meaning of the text. Boda is an expert on the texts as witnessed by his more academic research. He also has the sensitivities of a pastor, so his discussions of the contemporary significance of the text are very valuable. He has an excellent sense of theology and biblical theology. LM★★★★★

Craigie, P. C. *Twelve Prophets*. 2 vols. DSB. Westminster John Knox, 1985. ix/239 pp. and 272 pp.

See under Hosea.

Floyd, M. H. *Minor Prophets, Part 2*. FOTL. Eerdmans, 2000. xviii/641 pp.

See under Nahum.

Meyers, C. L., and E. M. Meyers. *Haggai; Zechariah 1–8*. AYBC. Yale University Press, 1987. xcv/478 pp.

The Meyers treat Haggai and Zechariah 1–8 not only as stemming from the same period of time, but also as two parts of the same composite work. (They will treat the latter part of Zechariah in a subsequent commentary; see below under Zechariah.) The Meyers are archaeologists, so their commentary is full of helpful historical and archaeological comments. The authors include an excellent bibliography. MS★★★★

Motyer, J. A. "Haggai." In *The Minor Prophets: An Exegetical and Expository Commentary*. Ed. T. McComiskey. Vol. 3. Baker, 1998. Pp. 963–1002.

Good solid exposition, though very short. Motyer also has apologetic interests in the forefront as he counters various critical ideas. He is particularly adamant about Haggai having been his own editor. LM★★★

Petersen, D. L. *Haggai and Zechariah*. OTL. Westminster John Knox/SCM, 1984. 320 pp.

Petersen and the Meyers have much in common in their approach to the text. They are both critical in their understanding of historical questions, but neither gets bogged down completely in such issues. Petersen is more interested in a positive interpretation of the books than in exhaustive interaction with the secondary literature. Like the Meyers, he does an admirable job reconstructing the historical, sociological, archaeological, and economic background to the text. MS★★★★

Redditt, P. L. *Haggai, Zechariah, Malachi*. NCB. Sheffield, 1995. 196 pp.

A short, readable commentary on these postexilic books. Redditt looks at the compositional history of these books in his introductions and provides historical background. The commentary proper focuses on the text itself. LM★★★

Smith, R. L. *Micah–Malachi*. WBC. Nelson/Paternoster, 1984. xvii/358 pp.

See under Micah.

Taylor, R. A., and E. R. Clendenen. *Haggai, Malachi*. NAC. Broadman, 2004. 496 pp.

See also under Malachi. Taylor wrote the commentary on Haggai, and it is a very serious, well-researched exposition of the book. The prose and the footnotes may get a bit heavy for laypeople, but ministers and scholars will appreciate the reflection and the interaction with other scholars. MS★★★✔

Verhoef, P. A. *The Books of Haggai and Malachi*. NICOT. Eerdmans, 1987. 384 pp.

Verhoef is a South African scholar who is considerably at home in postexilic literature. He does a careful job of exegeting the Hebrew text. He also explores the theological message of Haggai and Malachi and traces their themes into the New Testament. This commentary is more academic in style than many others in the NICOT series; thus, it is recommended as a scholarly guide to both of these prophetic books. MS★★★

Wolff, H. W. *Haggai*. CC. Fortress, 1988. 128 pp.

Wolff, as usual, is clear, concise, and insightful. He sees Haggai as a "model of communication." After all, Haggai was the one who got the Israelites to rebuild the temple. Wolff analyzes the book as the result of three "growth rings": Haggai's proclamation, the work of a Haggai chronicler, and interpolations. MS★★★★

ZECHARIAH

Achtemeier, E. *Nahum–Malachi*. Interp. Westminster John Knox, 1986. x/201 pp.

See under Nahum.

Baldwin, J. G. *Haggai, Zechariah, Malachi*. TOTC. InterVarsity, 1972. 253 pp.

See under Haggai.

Barker, K. L. *Zechariah.* REBC 8. Zondervan, 2008. Pp. 721–833.

Barker has given a solid dispensationalist interpretation to the book of Zechariah. It does not grapple much with critical issues but provides a competent theological reading with some detailed grammatical notes. LM★★★

Boda, M. J. *Haggai, Zechariah.* NIVAC. Zondervan/Hodder & Stoughton, 2004. 576 pp.

See under Haggai.

Craigie, P. C. *Twelve Prophets.* 2 vols. DSB. Westminster John Knox, 1985. ix/239 pp. and 272 pp.

See under Hosea.

Floyd, M. H. *Minor Prophets, Part 2.* FOTL. Eerdmans, 2000. xviii/641 pp.

See under Nahum.

McComiskey, T. "Zechariah." In *The Minor Prophets: An Exegetical and Expository Commentary.* Ed. T. McComiskey. Vol. 3. Baker, 1998. Pp. 1003–1244.

McComiskey gives a very reasonable and interesting exposition of the book from a conservative perspective. He recognizes the issues connected with seeing chapters 9–14 as not part of the original Zecharian composition, but resists simply cutting these chapters off. He is a sensitive reader of the literary images and a very competent linguist. LM★★★★

Meyers, C. L., and E. M. Meyers. *Haggai; Zechariah 1–8.* AYBC. Yale University Press, 1987. *Zechariah 9–14.* AYBC. Yale University Press, 1993. xcv/478 pp. and xxiii/552 pp.

See also under Haggai. The Anchor Yale Bible really has done it right with the Minor Prophets. They have apparently given the authors of all the volumes considerable latitude in length, and the Meyers have used their freedom with great success. This is a wonderfully written and researched commentary that I have found extremely provocative and largely persuasive. MS★★★★★

Petersen, D. L. *Haggai and Zechariah*. OTL. Westminster John Knox/SCM, 1984. 320 pp.

See under Haggai.

Petersen, D. L. *Zechariah 9–14 and Malachi*. OTL. Westminster John Knox/SCM, 1995. xxi/233 pp.

See under Malachi.

Redditt, P. L. *Haggai, Zechariah, Malachi*. NCB. Sheffield, 1995. 196 pp.

See under Haggai.

Smith, R. L. *Micah–Malachi*. WBC. Nelson/Paternoster, 1984. xvii/358 pp.

See under Micah.

MALACHI

Achtemeier, E. *Nahum–Malachi*. Interp. Westminster John Knox, 1986. x/201 pp.

See under Nahum.

Baker, D. W. *Joel, Obadiah, Malachi*. NIVAC. Zondervan/Hodder & Stoughton, 2006. 341 pp.

See under Joel.

Baldwin, J. G. *Haggai, Zechariah, Malachi*. TOTC. InterVarsity, 1972. 253 pp.

See under Haggai.

Craigie, P. C. *Twelve Prophets*. 2 vols. DSB. Westminster John Knox, 1985. ix/239 pp. and 272 pp.

See under Hosea.

Floyd, M. H. *Minor Prophets, Part 2*. FOTL. Eerdmans, 2000. xviii/641 pp.

See under Nahum.

Hill, A. E. *Malachi*. AYBC. Yale University Press, 1998. xliii/436 pp.

Hill provides an extensive and excellent analysis of the introductory issues connected with this book. His exposition of the book itself is also of high quality. The lay reader is forewarned that his writing and approach are fairly technical, even for the series. This is also one of the few volumes in this series that takes seriously connections with the New Testament. MS★★★★

Kaiser, W. C., Jr. *Malachi: God's Unchanging Love*. Baker, 1984. 171 pp.

A practical commentary that combines scholarly tidbits with pastoral concern. The volume illustrates principles found in the author's *Toward an Exegetical Theology*. An appendix on how to use commentaries is included. LM★★★

Merrill, E. H. *Malachi*. REBC 8. Zondervan, 2008. Pp. 835–63.

Merrill provides an excellent presentation of the message of Malachi, demonstrating his special interest in historical issues, though he does a good job at presenting the theology of the book in a concise fashion. LM★★★✓

Petersen, D. L. *Zechariah 9–14 and Malachi*. OTL. Westminster John Knox/SCM, 1995. xxi/233 pp.

Petersen treats these chapters as three different oracles, each initiated by the Hebrew word *massa'*. He dates all three of the oracles to the Persian period. He emphasizes historical background and sociological analysis. He also discusses at length form-critical and redaction-critical issues, but he is not strong on other types of literary analysis or theological contributions. S★★★

Redditt, P. L. *Haggai, Zechariah, Malachi*. NCB. Sheffield, 1995. 196 pp.

See under Haggai.

Smith, R. L. *Micah–Malachi*. WBC. Nelson/Paternoster, 1984. xvii/358 pp.

See under Micah.

Stuart, D. "Malachi." In *The Minor Prophets: An Exegetical and Expository Commentary*. Ed. T. McComiskey. Vol. 3. Baker, 1998. Pp. 1245–396.

This commentary is particularly good in connecting the prophet to covenant curses and blessings. It sometimes is overly apologetic, as when it argues against the possibility that Malachi stands for "my messenger" rather than being a proper name. LM★★★

Taylor, R. A., and E. R. Clendenen. *Haggai, Malachi*. NAC. Broadman, 2004. 496 pp.

See also under Haggai. Clendenen provided this meaty, helpful guide to the study of Malachi. He is up-to-date on his research and insightful on the text. He does an excellent job situating the book in its historical and economic context. MS★★★✔

Verhoef, P. A. *The Books of Haggai and Malachi*. NICOT. Eerdmans, 1987. 384 pp.

See under Haggai.

Appendix A

Five-Star Commentaries

The following commentaries received the highest ratings for each of the biblical books. These may not be the commentaries for you (for instance, they may be too technical or too critical), but they are the best because they accomplish their intentions from their own theological perspective most successfully.

ONE-VOLUME COMMENTARIES

Burge, G. M., and A. E. Hill, eds. *The Baker Illustrated Bible Commentary*. Baker Books, 2012. 1648 pp.

Carson, D. A., R. T. France, J. A. Motyer, and G. J. Wenham, eds. *New Bible Commentary: Twenty-First Century Edition*. InterVarsity, 1994. 1455 pp.

Walton, J. H., V. H. Matthews, and M. W. Chavalas. *The IVP Bible Background Commentary: Old Testament*. InterVarsity, 2000. 832 pp.

COMMENTARY SERIES

Ancient Christian Commentary on Scripture: Old Testament (ACCS). Ed. T. C. Oden. InterVarsity.

*Apollos Old Testament Commentary (AOTC). Ed. D. W. Baker and G. J. Wenham. InterVarsity.

*Baker Commentary on the Old Testament: Wisdom and Psalms (BCOTWP). Ed. T. Longman III. Baker Academic.

Calvin's Commentaries. 22 vols. Reprint, Baker.

*Hermeneia. Ed. F. M. Cross et al. Fortress/SCM.

*JPS Torah Commentary. Ed. N. M. Sarna. Jewish Publication Society.

The Minor Prophets. Ed. T. McComiskey. Baker.

*New International Version Application Commentary (NIVAC). Ed. A. Dearman, R. Hubbard, T. Longman III, and J. H. Walton. Zondervan/Hodder & Stoughton.

Zondervan Illustrated Bible Backgrounds Commentary. Ed. J. H. Walton. Zondervan, 2009.

INDIVIDUAL COMMENTARIES

Waltke, B. K., and C. J. Fredricks. *Genesis*. Zondervan, 2001. 656 pp.

Enns, P. *Exodus*. NIVAC. Zondervan/Hodder & Stoughton, 2000. 448 pp.

Hartley, J. E. *Leviticus*. WBC. Nelson/Paternoster, 1992. lxxiii/496 pp.

Hess, R. S. *Leviticus*. REBC 1. Zondervan, 2008. Pp. 563–825.

Kiuchi, N. *Leviticus*. AOTC. InterVarsity, 2007. 538 pp.

Milgrom, J. *Leviticus 1–16*. AYBC. Yale University Press, 1991. *Leviticus 17–22*. AYBC. Yale University Press, 2000. *Leviticus 23–27*.

AYBC. Yale University Press, 2001. xviii/1163 pp., xvii/624 pp., and xxi/818 pp.

Wenham, G. J. *The Book of Leviticus*. NICOT. Eerdmans, 1979. xiii/362 pp.

Cole, R. D. *Numbers*. NAC. Broadman, 2001. 590 pp.

Milgrom, J. *Numbers*. JPS Torah Commentary. Jewish Publication Society, 1990. lxi/520 pp.

Olson, D. T. *Numbers*. Interp. Westminster John Knox, 1996. 196 pp.

Hess, R. S. *Joshua*. TOTC. InterVarsity, 1996. 320 pp.

Hubbard, R. L., Jr. *Joshua*. NIVAC. Zondervan, 2009. 652 pp.

Block, D. I. *Judges, Ruth*. NAC. Broadman, 1999. 765 pp.

Boda, M. J. *Judges*. REBC 2. Zondervan, forthcoming.

Butler, T. *Judges*. WBC. Nelson, 2009. xcii/538 pp.

Bush, F. W. *Ruth/Esther*. WBC. Nelson/Paternoster, 1996. xiv/514 pp.

Hubbard, R. L., Jr. *The Book of Ruth*. NICOT. Eerdmans, 1988. xiv/317 pp.

Firth, D. G. *1 and 2 Samuel*. AOTC. InterVarsity, 2009. 614 pp.

Provan, I. W. *1 and 2 Kings*. UBCS. Baker Books, 1995. xiv/306 pp.

Dillard, R. B. *II Chronicles*. WBC. Nelson/Paternoster, 1987. xxiii/323 pp.

Japhet, S. *I and II Chronicles*. OTL. Westminster John Knox/SCM, 1993. xxv/1077 pp.

Williamson, H. G. M. *Ezra–Nehemiah*. WBC. Nelson/Paternoster, 1985. xix/428 pp.

Berlin, A. *Esther*. JPS Bible Commentary. Jewish Publication Society, 2001. lix/110 pp.

Jobes, K. *Esther*. NIVAC. Zondervan/Hodder & Stoughton, 1999. 248 pp.

Grogan, G. W. *Psalms*. THOTC. Eerdmans, 2008. xi/490 pp.

VanGemeren, W. *Psalms*. REBC 5. Zondervan, 2008. 863 pp.

Wilson, G. H. *Psalms*. Vol. 1. NIVAC. Zondervan/Hodder & Stoughton, 2002. 1024 pp.

Fox, M. V. *Proverbs 1–9*. AYBC. Yale University Press, 2000. xix/474 pp.

Waltke, B. K. *Proverbs 1–15*. NICOT. Eerdmans, 2004. *Proverbs 16–31*. NICOT. Eerdmans, 2005. 693 pp. and 589 pp.

Bartholomew, C. *Ecclesiastes*. BCOTWP. Baker Academic, 2009. 448 pp.

Oswalt, J. N. *Isaiah*. NIVAC. Zondervan/Hodder & Stoughton, 2003. 736 pp.

Sweeney, M. A. *Isaiah 1–39 with an Introduction to Prophetic Literature*. FOTL. Eerdmans, 1996. xix/547 pp.

Fretheim, T. E. *Jeremiah*. SHBC. Smyth and Helwys, 2002. 684 pp.

Lundbom, J. R. *Jeremiah 1–20*. AYBC. Yale University Press, 1999. *Jeremiah 21–36*. AYBC. Yale University Press, 2004. *Jeremiah 37–52*. AYBC. Yale University Press, 2004. 934 pp., 649 pp., and 624 pp.

Berlin, A. *Lamentations: A Commentary*. OTL. Westminster John Knox/SCM, 2002. xxvi/135 pp.

Parry, R. A. *Lamentations*. THOTC. Eerdmans, 2010. xii/260 pp.

Provan, I. *Lamentations*. NCB. Sheffield/Marshall Pickering, 1991. 134 pp.

Block, D. I. *The Book of Ezekiel 1–24*. NICOT. Eerdmans, 1997. *The Book of Ezekiel 25–48*. NICOT. Eerdmans, 1998. xxi/887 pp. and xxiii/826 pp.

Duguid, I. *Ezekiel*. NIVAC. Zondervan/Hodder & Stoughton, 1999. 568 pp.

Collins, J. J. *Daniel*. Hermeneia. Fortress/SCM, 1993. 498 pp.

Dearman, J. A. *The Book of Hosea*. NICOT. Eerdmans, 2010. xiv/408 pp.

McComiskey, T. "Hosea." In *The Minor Prophets: An Exegetical and Expository Commentary*. Ed. T. McComiskey. Vol. 1. Baker, 1992. Pp. 1–237.

Dillard, R. B. "Joel." In *The Minor Prophets: An Exegetical and Expository Commentary*. Ed. T. McComiskey. Vol. 1. Baker, 1992. Pp. 239–313.

Paul, S. M. *Amos*. Hermeneia. Fortress/SCM, 1991. xxvii/406 pp.

Raabe, P. R. *Obadiah*. AYBC. Yale University Press, 1996. xxvi/310 pp.

Sasson, J. M. *Jonah*. AYBC. Yale University Press, 1990. xvi/368 pp.

Walton, J. H. *Jonah*. REBC 8. Zondervan, 2008. Pp. 451–99.

Baker, D. W., T. D. Alexander, and B. K. Waltke. *Obadiah, Jonah, Micah*. TOTC. InterVarsity, 1988. 207 pp.

Waltke, B. K. *A Commentary on Micah*. Eerdmans, 2007. xviii/490 pp.

Waltke, B. K. "Micah." In *The Minor Prophets: An Exegetical and Expository Commentary*. Ed. T. McComiskey. Vol. 2. Baker, 1993. Pp. 591–764.

Berlin, A. *Zephaniah*. AYBC. Yale University Press, 1994. xvi/165 pp.

Boda, M. J. *Haggai, Zechariah*. NIVAC. Zondervan/Hodder & Stoughton, 2004. 576 pp.

Floyd, M. H. *Minor Prophets, Part 2*. FOTL. Eerdmans, 2000. xviii/641 pp.

Meyers, C. L., and E. M. Meyers. *Haggai; Zechariah 1–8*. AYBC. Yale University Press, 1987. *Zechariah 9–14*. AYBC. Yale University Press, 1993. xcv/478 pp. and xxiii/552 pp.

Appendix B

Commentaries by Tremper Longman III

Job. BCOTWP. Baker Academic, 2012. 496 pp.

Proverbs. BCOTWP. Baker Academic, 2006. 592 pp.

"Ecclesiastes." In *Job, Ecclesiastes, Song of Songs.* A. Konkel and T. Longman III. CsBC. Tyndale, 2006. 400 pp.

Ecclesiastes. NICOT. Eerdmans, 1998. xvi/306 pp.

"Song of Songs." In *Job, Ecclesiastes, Song of Songs.* A. Konkel and T. Longman III. CsBC. Tyndale, 2006. 400 pp.

Song of Songs. NICOT. Eerdmans, 2001. xvi/238 pp.

Jeremiah, Lamentations. UBCS. Baker Books, 2008. xvi/412 pp.

Daniel. NIVAC. Zondervan/Hodder & Stoughton, 1999. 313 pp.

"Nahum." In *The Minor Prophets: An Exegetical and Expository Commentary.* Ed. T. McComiskey. Vol. 2. Baker, 1993. Pp. 765–829.

Name Index

Italic page numbers indicate entries without annotations.